THE
INSOMNIA
BOOK

THE
DR. CHRIS IDZIKOWSKI
INSOMNIA
BOOK

Everything You Need for a Good Night's Sleep

FOREWORD BY

Wallace B. Mendelson, M.D.
UNIVERSITY OF CHICAGO SLEEP RESEARCH LABORATORY

PENGUIN
STUDIO

To Hilary, Liam, Kim, Dawn and Springfield

PENGUIN STUDIO
Published by the Penguin Group
Penguin Putnam Inc., 375 Hudson Street,
New York, New York 10014, U.S.A.
Penguin Books Ltd, 27 Wrights Lane,
London W8 5TZ, England
Penguin Books Australia Ltd, Ringwood,
Victoria, Australia
Penguin Books Canada Ltd, 10 Alcorn Avenue,
Toronto, Ontario, Canada M4V 3B2
Penguin Books (N.Z.) Ltd, 182–190 Wairau Road,
Auckland 10, New Zealand
Penguin India, 210 Chiranjiv Tower, 43 Nehru Place,
New Delhi 11009, India

Penguin Books Ltd, Registered Offices:
Harmondsworth, Middlesex, England

First published in the United States of America in 1999 by Penguin Studio,
a member of Penguin Putnam Inc.

1 3 5 7 9 10 8 6 4 2

CIP data available
ISBN 0-670-88255-0

AN EDDISON • SADD EDITION
Edited, designed and produced by
Eddison Sadd Editions Limited
St Chad's House, 148 King's Cross Road
London WC1X 9DH

Text copyright © Dr. Chris Idzikowski 1999
Line artwork copyright © Julie Carpenter 1999
Illustrations copyright © Steve Rawlings 1999
This edition copyright © Eddison Sadd Editions Limited 1999

Phototypeset in Joanna MT and Humanist 521 BT using QuarkXPress
on Apple Macintosh. Origination by Scanhouse, Malaysia.
Printed and bound by Sun Sang Printing Products Ltd, Hong Kong.

Contents

Foreword

If you have trouble sleeping, you are not alone. About one third of the population has difficulty sleeping, and just under a third of them—roughly one person in ten—considers it a major problem in their life. Insomnia is not just trouble sleeping at night. It is associated with decreased ability to work effectively during the day, memory troubles, and reduced ability to enjoy being with family and friends. People with insomnia are also more likely to have automobile accidents due to sleepiness. Evidence shows that people who have poor sleep achieve less, and keep jobs for less time, than those with undisturbed sleep. So the discomfort of lying in bed awake is just one of many reasons why it is important to sleep well.

Fortunately there are a number of things you can do for yourself to help improve your sleep. Dr. Chris Idzikowski has provided a very helpful guide to aid you along the way. It begins by helping you learn a little bit about what sleep is, and how it is regulated by your body. He then gives you an invaluable tool—the "sleep-awake ruler"—to help you measure your sleep and determine where the difficulties lie, using a 28-day sleep diary. You will discover how to deal with sleep that is disturbed for reasons out of your hands—for instance, if you are doing shift-work, or if events in your life go awry—and there are helpful techniques that you can use straight away. He also explains the disorders that can cause poor sleep, and when to seek help from a specialist. And there is advice on using complementary therapies, plus a list of resources, including his website, to provide further support.

You are taking an important first step on the path to good sleep, and I wish you a successful journey.

WALLACE B. MENDELSON, M.D., CHICAGO, 1998

Introduction

Sleeplessness can get out of control. This kit helps you to identify what is wrong, how to deal with it, and, if you can't deal with it yourself, where to go for help. Sleep research and medicine is a dynamic area: ideas, treatments, and therapies change constantly. To keep up to date, a website has been set up so that you can access the latest developments (*see page 157 for details*).

I have been involved in research in the fields of psychology and clinical pharmacology for more than 20 years. This has meant that I have spent a lot of my time trying to bridge the gap between the physical and the mental. Sleep has been an important part of my work—partly because when someone is asleep his or her body and brain responds, for the most part, without the confusion of will, ideas, and so on, and partly because sleep itself is so complex and intensely interesting. Sleep is not just a simple shutdown of awareness. Much continues to work in both body and brain. The fringes of sleep—the states when awareness and sleep are competing to take control—are fascinating research areas.

I am often asked how I got involved with sleep. Do I have a sleep problem? Do I dream a lot? The answer is generally, no. I was about to start research into the auditory and visual systems when it turned out that my wife-to-be did not understand what I was doing (she typed out a project report for me). Since a book on sleep by Emeritus Professor Ian Oswald had already drawn me into this most fascinating area, I went instead to the sleep laboratory in Edinburgh University's Department of Psychiatry, where there happened to be a research opening. Since then, I have never left the area of sleep.

About this book

This book is contemporary in the use of clinical and research knowledge, but it is my own view of sleep research and sleep medicine, evolved over twenty or so years. Nearly everyone has lost the ability to sleep at one time or another. Clinically, sleep disorders can be devastating. Sleepiness, particularly uncontrolled and unexpected sleepiness, can lead to accidents and poor decisions; sleeplessness can ruin a person's quality of life.

This book looks at sleep, disturbed sleep, disordered sleep, and sleep disorders. It explains sleep, identifies the problems, and suggests remedies. These remedies range from over-the-counter sleep aids and general advice on lifestyle, to relaxation techniques that can be used to alleviate anxiety. Complementary therapies that may be of help are also discussed.

A fundamental part of this kit is based on a diary that I devised for the Sleep Assessment and Advisory Service in the UK. The Service was designed to be used at long range by doctors who want advice concerning their patients. This book is a natural extension of the Service: it allows you to make your own assessment.

Know your sleep!

Early in 1998, the US National Sleep Foundation conducted a telephone survey of more than a thousand Americans to assess their knowledge about sleep. Only 14 percent passed the Sleep IQ test. Many were found to believe risky myths about sleep, and 23 percent acknowledged that they had fallen asleep whilst driving in the previous year. Some of the myths were:
• The older you get, the fewer hours of sleep you need.
• Raising the volume on the radio will help you stay awake while driving.
• The human body is able to successfully adjust to night-shift work.
• Snoring is not harmful as long as it doesn't disturb the body's need for sleep.

Nearly one in three Americans has been found to sleep six hours or less during the working week, despite rating his or her sleep as important as nutrition and exercise. The

8

average sleep adults require before becoming sleepy is around seven-and-a-half hours, so many working Americans are not getting enough sleep. The National Highway Traffic Safety Administration reports that there are at least 100,000 crashes in the US annually directly caused by drowsy drivers, and about 1,500 of these are fatal. Sleep is as important as wakefulness: this kit provides the basic information to enable you to deal with your sleep sensibly.

How to use this kit

There are various ways to use this kit. You can read the book, using the diary and tape as you get to them, or you can read the book on its own first. The first two chapters explain how sleep works and how you can "measure" your sleep using the sleep-awake ruler. Chapter Three offers advice on how to manage your sleep by taking account of the various factors that affect it, and Chapter Four shows you how to cope when sleep needs to fit into the demands of your life.

Chapter Five includes the 28-day sleep diary. I recommend that you fill this in for 14 days, complete the assessments in Chapter Five and read the advice on dealing with sleep disorders in Chapter Six, and then return to the diary to fill in the remaining 14 days. You will then be able to see if there has been any improvement in your sleep. Chapter Six also introduces the tape, which includes a breathing exercise, a guided visualization, and a mantra to aid relaxation and alleviate anxiety and stress, plus a progressive relaxation routine specifically designed to help you go to sleep. Chapter Seven covers major sleep disorders including, among others, specific insomnias, nightmares, and sleepwalking, while Chapter Eight outlines a variety of complementary therapies that can help with insomnia or sleep disorders.

Together, this book and tape will show you how to get a good night's sleep.

Chapter One

So you think you're an insomniac?

This chapter, and the two following, deal with sleep basics. At the end of them you should have a better idea about the nature of sleep, and how to control it, and also an understanding about whether or not you have a sleep problem.

The National Commission on Sleep Disorders Research noted that over sixty million Americans are affected by insomnia each year. Between 30 and 35 percent experience insomnia at least once a year, and 15 percent judge their problem as serious. Many millions more suffer from disturbed sleep that they do not describe as insomnia, and that they do not complain about.

Minor problems can turn into long-term problems, so it's worth tackling them quickly. If the princess in the Hans Christian Andersen fairy-tale really couldn't sleep on top of twenty mattresses and twenty feather beds because there was a pea on the bottom bed, then we need to look at why she became so sensitive in the first place. In the same way, chronic insomniacs may have something in their past that started as a small problem and turned into a big one.

Research has shown that even minor sleep disturbances, so minor that the sleeper does not wake up and is not even aware of any disturbance, will cause daytime performance problems and possibly sleepiness.

From sleeplessness 1894 to insomnia today

Many people complain that life is tougher, faster, and more fraught than it ever used to be, so it is no surprise people have difficulty sleeping. This may not be correct, as the following quotation from the *British Medical Journal* shows:

The subject of sleeplessness is once more under public discussion. The hurry and excitement of modern life is quite correctly held to be responsible for much of the insomnia of which we hear: and most of the articles and letters are full of good advice to live more quietly and of platitudes concerning the harmfulness of rush and worry. The pity of it is that so many people are unable to follow this good advice and are obliged to lead a life of anxiety and high tension. Hence the search for some sovereign panacea that will cure the evil. Many are the remedies suggested: hot baths, cold baths, hot drinks, cold drinks, long walks before retiring to rest, and so forth. Different remedies suit different cases . . . To be read off to sleep by a gentle voice is, perhaps, the pleasantest way.

September 29, 1894, British Medical Journal 719

This was written more than 100 years ago, yet it could have been written today.

In order to understand sleep problems it is useful to understand how sleep relates to physiology. In many countries, the primary treatment of insomnia by the medical profession is through the prescription of sleeping pills (also known as hypnotics). Many people also try to treat themselves by using alcohol, or over-the-counter sleep preparations. But using a medicine just to treat a symptom is like using a hammer to fix a TV set. If you are lucky it may work the first time, but next time you might break the TV!

Brain and mind

We do not understand much about the mind or the brain, but I will put forward my own particular views, based on more than 20 years of research in the area, so that you can start to get to grips with how your sleep is affected by both biological and mental events. I am going to leave out theorists and practitioners such as Freud, because there is not enough space in this book to examine their ideas, but we need to do some work on the brain and the mind. There now follows the shortest course in neuroscience and philosophy that you are ever likely to come across.

Brain

The end of the nineteenth century and the beginning of the twentieth saw a lot of progress in the field of neurology, the medical science that deals with problems associated with the nervous system. It became apparent that there were centers in the brain that controlled wakefulness. If those centers were not active then a person would become unresponsive (not necessarily asleep).

Sleeping sickness, otherwise known as epidemic lethargic encephalitis, provided many of the clues. It not only causes extreme sleepiness, but also at other times extreme sleeplessness. It can switch around the usual light–dark, activity–rest pattern. Patients remain awake during the night and asleep during the day. The condition was not investigated thoroughly until a major epidemic during the First World War, when the Austrian neurologist Von Economo (who discovered the disease) described the specific brain centers that were involved with the control of wakefulness and sleep.

The film *Awakenings* has increased awareness of epidemic lethargic encephalitis. It describes the use of the medicine L-dopa in the "awakening" of a number of patients who had remained trapped in a rigid and inarticulate state for many years. L-dopa is a substance that occurs naturally in the body—one of the neurotransmitters (brain chemical messengers) that control the awake and sleep states.

This shows how the sleep, awake, and clock systems interact when you are awake. For normal sleep to take place, the sleep system needs to be active, and the awake system switched off.

Key

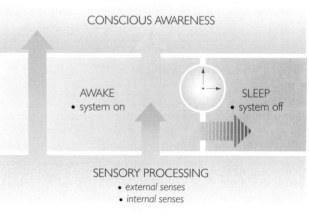

Mental World

CONSCIOUS AWARENESS

AWAKE
• system on

SLEEP
• system off

SENSORY PROCESSING
• *external senses*
• *internal senses*

Physical World

facilitates activity

inhibits activity

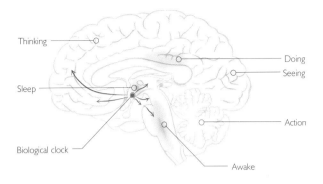

Thinking

Doing

Seeing

Sleep

Action

Biological clock

Awake

This section through the brain shows the rough location of the main centers, including the sleep, awake, and clock centers.

The main point is that sleep is an active brain state, and that without specific sleep centers working properly, and wake centers able to shut down, sleep cannot take place. The diagram below left shows how these systems might interact. It also shows a "clock." The existence of clock systems has only become apparent in the last 30 years. The clock is connected to the awake system—as well as the sleep system—but this is controversial. This biological clock (named the suprachiasmatic nucleus) although small, has a huge number of connections throughout the brain, some of which connect to the sleep systems.

Shown above is a slice through the human brain, indicating the rough locations of the main "centers." The "clock" center is located in the hypothalamus, which is also involved in the regulation of eating, drinking, and sex. The "sleep" center is located in a region that is also involved with the control of body temperature. The regions involved in the control of sleep, awake, and clock, are not located in areas that are easy to control by voluntary methods. Animals with electrodes implanted in the right parts of the brain can be trained to sleep on command by using conditioning techniques, but this is not a technique that can readily be used on people!

Mind

Sleep is a state that can be recognized in many animals, but in man it is nevertheless a state of mind, or non-mind. The sleep-awake and clock centers interact with higher centers in the brain and inevitably must interact with the mind.

Most neuroscientists argue that the pattern of nerve cell (neuron) firing is a mental state. The estimates for the number of neurons in the human brain range from 10 billion to 1 trillion. Recent work estimates that out of about 85 billion, 12–15 billion are involved with those areas of the brain that deal with higher functions such as thinking and personality; 70 billion with control of movement and musculature, and about 1 billion are in the brainstem and spinal neurons. The brainstem is the lower part of the brain that connects the spinal cord with the brain. This is also the area that contains parts of the "awake" center. Even if you consider only the raw numbers, without considering the connections between the neurons, and the fact that neurons have more than one connection (some may have thousands), then you can imagine that even with current technology we are nowhere near achieving a simulation of any mental state on a computer.

The suprachiasmatic nucleus (biological clock) consists of only 12–15,000 neurons, yet its effects can be very powerful. For some people, jet lag is their first experience of not being able to control sleep on demand (it never was on demand, but their sleep could mold itself to their lifestyle) and the biological clock is a major factor in causing this. Mind and consciousness are inseparable, but curiously, though mind may go to sleep, it is rare to see any discussion concerning sleep in contemporary debates on mind and consciousness.

The table shown below outlines possible levels of consciousness and also serves as a reminder of various common waking experiences that are not simply involved with

There are a number of different levels of consciousness, and the higher levels are related to various common waking experiences.

Levels of consciousness	Waking experiences
Conscious self-awareness	• Deliberate inner speech
Conscious awareness	• Deliberate recall
Alert awareness	• Recalled mental images
	• Driving without attention
Sleepy awareness	• Day dreaming
Automatic skills	• Inattention
Reactivity	• Reality aware
Reflex	• Inner voice or someone else's?
Autonomic	• Environment or location aware

thinking. Autonomic systems, that control functions such as heart rate, basic breathing, and sweating do not appear to sleep. Many reflexes such as the knee-jerk are inhibited during sleep. General reactivity goes down. This varies depending on the stage of sleep (*see page 25*).

Sleepy awareness refers to that twilight time when someone is not yet fully asleep and still has some idea what is going on around them. Automatic skills refer to highly learned simple movements that do not demand attention, for example turning the pillow over.

Alert awareness, conscious awareness and conscious self-awareness are in the domain of consciousness. To distinguish man from animals, debates take place as to whether animals are aware of themselves. Sleep clearly affects the higher levels shown in the table, and to a lesser extent the lower levels. This does not necessarily mean that processing to support the higher levels stops during sleep; it might just be the awareness of self-processing.

Most sleep research does not deal with consciousness, certainly not with this level of detail. This is partly because it is not possible to ask many of these questions in laboratory experiments and with animals it is difficult, although not impossible, to define the level of consciousness. It is possible to ask questions dealing with alertness, and the ability to respond, and to quantify the changes.

Brain, mind and sleep

The main points of the above are that sleep depends on both brain and mind. If the sleep, awake or clock centers are biologically damaged (by using common drugs such as caffeine or alcohol, or drugs of abuse, or by strokes, injury, age, and so on) then sleep will be disturbed. Equally, sleep will not come if the mind is upset. Disturbed sleep can be either neuronic (based on neurons) or neurotic (based on mental state). Neuronic theories include all hormonal and other biological influences on sleep. In 1895, one of the ideas circulating among physiologists was that the neurons shrank during sleep. The idea was that shrinkage broke the connecting pathways between neurons and sleep ensued. Neurotic theories do not imply mental disorder, they just define the mental structures involved in sleep. Dr Phil Barnard (Medical Research Council, UK) suggests that sleep is a state when "self" moves into a state of existential safety by suspension of focal awareness. This is achieved when a number of mental variables—body status, safety, control, "self"status, and goal-status—reach a specific threshold.

Unfortunately, the important neural or mental components cannot be measured easily. So this book approaches the problem of sleep disorder by measuring and describing objective and subjective sleep, and by examining all the variables that we know affect sleep. The sleep-awake-clock model is then used to describe what may be going wrong and how to remedy the problem or problems.

What is sleep? Sleep is usually defined as a time when an animal stops responding to its surroundings. Most animals close their eyes. Many adopt a specific posture—dogs and cats curl up, bats hang upside down. To distinguish sleep from coma and death, scientists note that this state is reversible!

With human beings, we are used to thinking of sleep as a time when we stop, more or less completely, being aware of anything. For some, it can be a sanctuary, a place to escape. For others, such as sleep apneics (*see page* 135) it is a nuisance, often making them drop off unexpectedly during the day. In others still, the boundaries between sleep and waking can be blurred.

What is normal sleep? There is no straightforward answer to this question, as sleep varies so much between individuals and with circumstances that it is difficult to give a precise answer. The time a person sleeps, the duration of the sleep, the continuity of the sleep and the recuperative value of the sleep is an amalgamation of various factors, including general health, habits, and family demands (*see page* 20). Normality needs biological, personal, and social frames of reference before an answer can be given. If you feel that there is something wrong with your sleep, and you do not feel well or cannot cope, and if the problem has been going on for several months, then read on.

In industrialized societies sleep is a compromise between biology and the demands of society—it is said that Thomas Edison created havoc by inventing the electric light bulb. There is evidence to suggest that normal sleep does not consist of one block of 7½ hours during the night. It is more likely that our biology is designed to allow us to sleep for about 6 hours during the night and 1½ hours during the day. The cultures where this pattern of sleep can be seen—the siesta cultures—have virtually disappeared (*see page* 34). Sleeping just once in 24 hours is called monophasic sleep, whereas broken sleep is polyphasic. In evolutionary terms, polyphasic animals are the most common, whereas monophasic animals have evolved more recently. Polyphasic patterns of sleep are the most common.

Nocturnal animals are generally active during the night but get some sleep; they sleep during the day but are also active. Diurnal (daytime) animals are more active during the day but also get lots of naps, and vice versa during the night. How well an animal can manage in its environment depends largely on the sense organs it uses. Animals that rely largely on the visual system are likely to be diurnal and will get most of their sleep during the night. Other influences such as satiety (how well fed the animal feels), body and brain temperature, the previous duration of wakefulness, and safe location all contribute to the likelihood of going to sleep. Whatever evolutionary advantage it might give, the mix of these factors results in the animal's habitual sleep pattern.

As societies have become more information-sensitive, the need to maintain high levels of awareness has gone up. Sleep obviously reduces awareness, but even naps are associated with periods of poor information processing. The constant demand for alertness during the day not only prevents daytime sleep, but also has an impact on night-time sleep. However, you only need to look at pre-school children, people on holiday, and the retired, to see sleep reappear during the day.

One piece of advice given in many magazine articles is not to nap during the day. I will return to this later (*see page*

When to sleep?

64) but it is worth noting that this is not necessarily good advice: it very much depends on the circumstances. Any sleep, however short, will reduce the pressure to sleep. In an ideal biological world napping (polyphasic) sleep might be best, as the body is never unduly stressed. This contrasts with monophasic sleep patterns where pressure builds to a maximum during wakefulness, and this sleep pressure is then reduced during sleep.

If an elderly person prefers to have a long daytime nap, and accepts that this means less sleep during the night, then that is fine (sorry, carers). It is the amount of sleep over a 24-hour period that is important, rather than the amount of sleep that takes place during the night.

How long should I sleep? Again, this is a common question. There is no straightforward answer because so many different factors need to be considered. However, you can say that good sleepers fall asleep quickly, and have serene, deep and uninterrupted sleep; they do not snore; they wake up feeling refreshed, and do not feel sleepy during the day; they feel that their sleep is enough (whatever it is).

Some people are constitutionally short sleepers (3½ to 4½ hours) but they do not usually complain about their short sleep if they feel well, and are not sleepy or tired during the day. They may be worried about sleeping so little, but there is no need to if they feel OK, and are satisfied with the way they are functioning. If they are happy with their lives, then the short sleep is a benefit, not a problem. They are probably happy because they are doing something productive, and have the edge on everyone else! It is very difficult to turn yourself into a short sleeper if your genetic make-up hasn't made you one.

In contrast, poor sleepers may snore and wake up more than once during the night. They may feel tired and sleepy, and drop off to sleep during the day; or they may feel tired but not be able to sleep during the day, as well as feeling irritable and miserable. You know if you are a poor sleeper.

In the 1950s the American Cancer Society conducted a survey to try to identify factors involved in the develop-

ment of cancers. This included a question about sleep duration. They found that the majority slept approximately 7½ hours, give or take 1½ hours. So, most of the population slept between 6 and 9 hours. Contemporary research, albeit with smaller numbers, suggests that there is much more pressure on Americans' sleep nowadays, and that work schedules, and possibly television, are reducing the amount of time allowed for sleep during the night.

A small reduction in total sleep may not matter too much, as the lighter stages of sleep tend to be lost if the amount of time allowed for sleep is habitually reduced. In adults, nearly half of sleep consists of light sleep, a quarter of deep sleep, and another quarter of REM (rapid eye movement, or dreaming) sleep. If you lose sleep one night, then the proportion of deep sleep and REM sleep increases the following night. Any deficit can be made up at weekends.

One study looked at nuns in a convent whose lifestyle forced them to have less sleep than the average. The nuns were given a dispensation to take part in the study, which allowed them to sleep as long as they liked in the morning. Their sleep rapidly moved back to the average, suggesting that even after years of training, it was impossible to learn to sleep less.

Sleep duration does not necessarily go down as you get older, but sleep is lighter and more fragmented (*see page 60 for more details*).

Long sleepers also feel that they have a problem, or in the case of adolescents, parents may feel that they have a problem. Ten or more hours' sleep is unusual, but not something to worry about. Greater than this, and it is useful to examine what is causing the extra sleep. If the sleepiness intrudes into the day then it should certainly be examined, as it may be pointing to disorders that are disturbing sleep during the night (*see page 134*).

The time taken to go to sleep is normally between 5 and 20 minutes. If it takes longer than 30 minutes, then people start to wonder what has gone wrong.

How long should it take to fall asleep?

How long should it take me to wake up? For most people, waking up is not an issue—the alarm clock goes off, and even if they feel (and look) like zombies, they get up and go. Experimental studies have shown though that it takes around 20 minutes to shake off sleep in the morning. This is called sleep inertia, and performance is affected during this time. If you always find it difficult to wake up, and you find that you always have difficulty going to bed and getting to sleep, then you might be suffering from a biological clock disorder called delayed-sleep-phase syndrome (*see page* 141).

How often should I dream? Provided the dreams are not nightmares, and are not leaving you drained, the maximum a person can dream depends on the amount of time spent in REM sleep (*see page* 26). The

Factors affecting sleep

A wide variety of factors can affect your sleep—some of which you may not even be aware of.

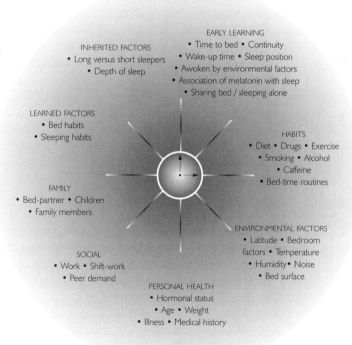

INHERITED FACTORS
• Long versus short sleepers
• Depth of sleep

EARLY LEARNING
• Time to bed • Continuity
• Wake-up time • Sleep position
• Awoken by environmental factors
• Association of melatonin with sleep
• Sharing bed / sleeping alone

LEARNED FACTORS
• Bed habits
• Sleeping habits

HABITS
• Diet • Drugs • Exercise
• Smoking • Alcohol
• Caffeine
• Bed-time routines

FAMILY
• Bed-partner • Children
• Family members

ENVIRONMENTAL FACTORS
• Latitude • Bedroom factors • Temperature
• Humidity • Noise
• Bed surface

SOCIAL
• Work • Shift-work
• Peer demand

PERSONAL HEALTH
• Hormonal status
• Age • Weight
• Illness • Medical history

ultradian cycle determines the timing of the dreams, so dreams could be expected every 90 minutes. What is not clear is who recalls their dreams. If a person is woken up in a sleep laboratory or a sleep disorders center in the REM stage, and asked what is going on in his or her mind, the sleeper is invariably dreaming. Awareness probably continues beyond the point marked asleep in the illustration on page 14, so how lightly you sleep is important. Also, the length of time between a dream finishing and waking up will contribute to the chances of recalling a dream.

Heredity has a major effect on sleep depth and duration. Also learned factors, both what your parents (grandparents, nanny or babysitter) did to you when you were a baby and a youngster, and what habits you have picked up over the years; environmental factors (bed, bedroom, latitude, season); and personal factors (good or poor health, menstrual cycle, menopause, age, and so on) all contribute to your sleep. (*See diagram left.*)

Factors affecting sleep

A vital feature of this book is the use of the sleep-awake ruler, explained in detail in the next chapter. Using it is the first step to logging what you are doing and what your sleep is doing. Most changes in sleep take time. Some of the changes can be progressive, like those associated with growing old. Others can be faster, changes within the seasons, the month, a week, or days. Some of the changes occur within one night. In order to understand and appreciate these changes yourself, you need to measure what is happening. Your memory is not good enough. Sleep affects memory, so you need to write down what is happening to you in some form of diary. The sleep-awake ruler is one way of doing this. (A 28-day blank diary with rulers is provided in Chapter Five.)

Sleep rulers

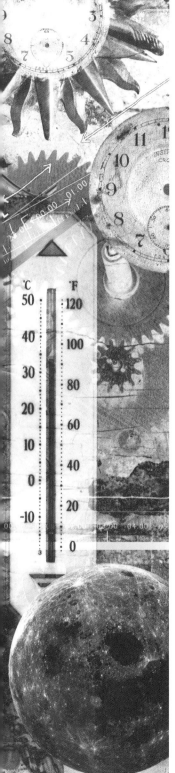

Chapter Two

How to measure sleep

Over the years I have measured sleep in various ways, using electroencephalography (EEG machines which measure brain activity using electrodes glued to the scalp) in laboratory settings, portable EEGs, actigraphy, various questionnaires and subjective ratings scales. For the past 4 years I have been using a particular form of sleep log, which I have called the sleep-awake ruler. It allows patients a convenient and fast way to describe what has happened to them during the night.

The sleep-awake ruler

The ruler is divided up into two 12-hour lengths. This is because displaying 24 hours on one ruler on one piece of paper is difficult, and the print may be too small for an elderly person to read. One ruler is for measuring, recording and displaying sleep during the night and the other one is for the day (*see above right*). The rulers are based on the 24-hour clock, so 1:00 pm becomes 13:00, 10:00 pm becomes 22:00, and so on.

The night ruler starts at 21:00 and finishes at 09:00, while the day ruler starts at 09.00 and finishes at 21.00. In order to record significant sleep events we need to use some symbols. These are shown in the sleep key on page 24.

The first ruler (*page 24*) shows what could be described as a normal night's sleep. The sleeper goes to bed around 22:45, and within a few minutes tries to go to sleep; falls asleep quickly, again within a few minutes; sleeps for around 7½ hours; wakes up, stays in bed for a few minutes, decides not to return to sleep, and gets up.

The second ruler (*page 24*) also shows a completed sleep ruler, but for someone who is having great difficulties with sleep. The sleeper goes to bed about 22:00, but does not

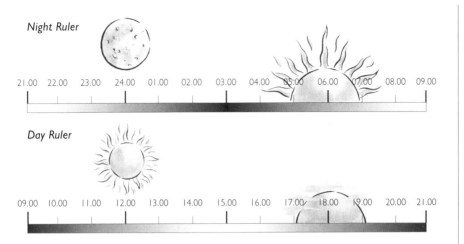

Night Ruler

21.00 22.00 23.00 24.00 01.00 02.00 03.00 04.00 05.00 06.00 07.00 08.00 09.00

Day Ruler

09.00 10.00 11.00 12.00 13.00 14.00 15.00 16.00 17.00 18.00 19.00 20.00 21.00

try to sleep until 23:00. He then takes nearly an hour to fall asleep, but wakes up again after about 1½ hours. Half an hour later he manages to get back to sleep, but it is a restless and disturbed sleep. Eventually, the sleeper settles down, but wakes up earlier than he had hoped. He stays in bed for another hour before giving up trying to sleep, but remains in bed anyway before getting up an hour later. By the end of this book, you will understand many of the reasons why this person's sleep is so disturbed.

Finally, the sleep rulers need to have additional notes to try to assess what factors are disturbing sleep. A few are listed on the right. A more comprehensive list and discussion are found in the diary section (*see pages 70–72*).

Now that the rulers have been introduced, they can be used to increase the precision of my description of sleep-awake mechanisms. The sleep onset diagram (*see page 25*) shows what happens to someone who takes a while to go to sleep. The sleeper goes to bed at a time when the awake system is beginning to run down. Most people as the evening progresses start routines that begin to relax and prepare them for the night's sleep. Coupled with this, and the connection is not clear, circadian clock activity (*see page 27*) is also optimized to allow sleep to take place. An index of this

Common sleep disturbers

- children
- dreaming
- toilet
- snoring partners
- restless partners
- partners who have other ideas than sleep
- room temperature
- uncomfortable bed/bedclothes
- noisy pets
- thinking
- worries

A normal night's sleep

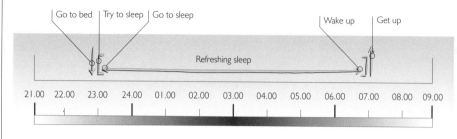

Go to bed | Try to sleep | Go to sleep   Wake up | Get up

Refreshing sleep

21.00 22.00 23.00 24.00 01.00 02.00 03.00 04.00 05.00 06.00 07.00 08.00 09.00

A difficult night's sleep

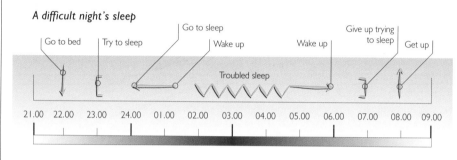

Go to sleep

Give up trying
to sleep

Go to bed | Try to sleep   Wake up   Wake up | Get up

Troubled sleep

21.00 22.00 23.00 24.00 01.00 02.00 03.00 04.00 05.00 06.00 07.00 08.00 09.00

Sleep key

↓	Going to bed (with the intention to sleep)
[	Start trying to sleep
←	Going to sleep
—	Tranquil and quiet sleep
↑	Getting up
]	Stop trying to sleep
⟹	Waking up
ᭌᭌ	Broken, wakeful sleep

is core body temperature. It has been found that most people go to sleep in the evening when this is decreasing (it usually peaks in the early evening). Core temperature runs on a 24-hour cycle, with the peak occurring early evening and the trough taking place early morning around dawn.

There is more happening than is shown in the sleep onset illustration. In the hours of darkness, melatonin is secreted from the pineal gland. Many other hormones secrete more or less during or prior to sleep—prolactin, testosterone, and thyroid-stimulating hormone. In fact, so many of the body's physiological systems are changing, that it is surprising how many people can fall asleep quickly and easily!

If you have not already started to wonder at how complicated sleep seems to be, it doesn't get any easier once you are asleep! Sleep is not continuous. You do not simply switch off, stay switched off, and then wake up. In adults, a 90-minute rhythm punctuates sleep. This rhythm seems to be dependent on brain size. Animals with small brains have a

24

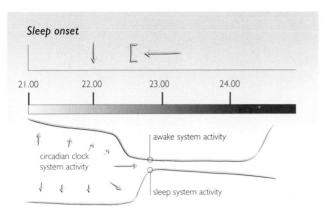

This person goes to bed as their awake system begins to wind down. As this happens, the activity of the circadian (biological) clock allows sleep to take place, and so the sleep system then begins to take over.

faster rhythm, for example mice at about 15 minutes; whereas animals with large brains have a slower rhythm (elephants at 100 minutes). Babies' rhythm is around 60 minutes and as the brain matures and enlarges the rhythm slows to the adult 90 minutes. This rhythm is called ultradian rhythm because it is shorter than the 24-hour circadian rhythm.

Stages of sleep

There are five sleep stages, shown below. The graph shows the average duration of each stage, while the EEGs show the brain activity, with further muscle and eye activity shown for REM sleep.

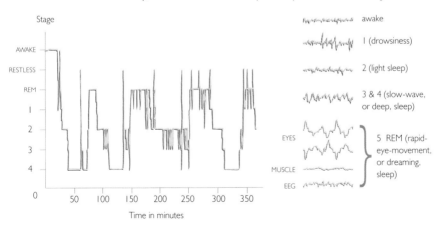

Ultradian rhythm This is an important rhythm for those with sleep problems because it punctuates sleep with wakefulness. It is known as the REM–REM cycle ultradian rhythm, because it is usually measured by determining the time from the onset of one bout of REM to the next. REM, or dreaming, does not just occur at the end of the night, but repeats itself. Usually, the first REM period is quite short (10–15 minutes) and it progressively lengthens during the night, so that it is more than 45 minutes by the end.

As sleep changes from light sleep to REM sleep, there can be periods of wakefulness. The diagram below uses the sleep ruler to illustrate someone who is continuously asleep for 7 hours, without apparent interruption. But the EEG (brain waves) would show interruptions to sleep. There might even be EEG wakefulness, but not long enough for either the sleeper to recall it, or for the sleep to be sufficiently impaired to result in daytime sleepiness. As you get older, the interruption becomes longer, and you may become aware that you are awake. If there are problems that you are worried about, and you start thinking about them, this may disrupt your sleep enough to prevent you from returning to sleep. For the elderly, medical conditions may also lighten sleep, so that these normal interruptions have an even greater impact on sleep.

The REM–REM cycle continues throughout sleep, each period of REM becoming progressively longer. The changeover from light sleep to REM sleep may cause wakefulness—even though the sleeper may not realize it.

The function of this rhythm is completely unknown. When it was first noted in the early days of sleep research, the suggestion was that mammals needed to awaken occasionally to check their surroundings for predators. Nathaniel

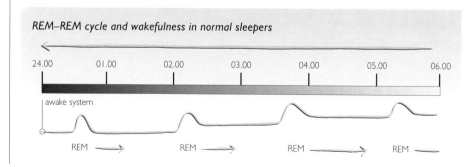

REM–REM cycle and wakefulness in normal sleepers

Kleitman, one of the most eminent researchers into sleep, advocated in the 1930s the existence of a basic rest-activity cycle. All animals, not just mammals, have a rest-activity cycle. There are various rhythms in adults that run roughly on a 70–90-minute cycle, such as respiration and digestive tract motility (*see page 30*). There is some evidence that these rhythms also affect other mental functions. Snacking behavior, for example, runs on a 90-minute cycle.

Circadian cycles

There are numerous 24-hour rhythms that are controlled by the circadian or biological clock, including the body temperature curve. Peak temperature occurs early in the evening. Generally, you fall asleep more easily when body temperature starts to go down. Lowest body temperature occurs in the early hours of the morning (around 04:00 for many people) and this is the time when it is easiest to fall asleep. Body temperature then rises until awakening. The body temperature rhythm and other cycles controlled by the biological clock are difficult, if not impossible, to control voluntarily. Difficulties with jet lag and shift-work are probably caused by the clock running at an inappropriate rate, causing difficulties in sleeping. Growth hormone has a 24-hour cycle that is strongly related to deep sleep, so peak secretion takes place early in the morning (*see below*).

The biological clock controls the rhythms of body temperature and growth hormone, both of which are related to sleep.

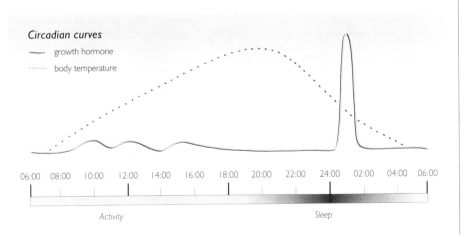

Circadian curves

—— growth hormone

········ body temperature

06:00 08:00 10:00 12:00 14:00 16:00 18:00 20:00 22:00 24:00 02:00 04:00 06:00

Activity   *Sleep*

27

Sleep Dynamics   When sleep is investigated using electroencephalograms (EEG), it is striking how dynamic a process it is. The brain does not simply switch off and lie dormant. It still reacts to the environment and the internal state of the body, and monitors sleep itself. If someone's sleep is disrupted, then various mechanisms come into play to try to compensate for the disturbance.

Sleep rebound   If someone is sleep-deprived, then the pressure for sleep increases. Normally, a healthy adult's sleep consists of roughly 25 percent deep sleep (slow-wave sleep), 25 percent REM sleep and 50 percent light sleep (stage 2). If you normally sleep for 8 hours a night, that would be 2 hours deep sleep and 2 hours REM sleep. If you are prevented from sleeping for 2 nights, do you require 24 hours continuous sleep to recover? Experience tells us this does not usually happen without the intervention of drugs or illness. Usually, deep sleep takes priority, followed by REM sleep. The first night is not completely taken up by the 4 hours of deep sleep that is missing (that would be 6 hours deep sleep altogether), but it does take up a substantial amount of that time. The rest of the first recovery night is primarily REM sleep. The second recovery night mops up most of the remaining deep sleep, and a lot of REM sleep is also recovered. As REM sleep is associated with dreaming, that can mean that some people experience a lot of dreaming. Sleep rebound means the compensatory increase in these stages on recovery nights. The only casualty is light sleep. This virtually disappears in the recovery nights and is lost. No function has ever been delegated to light sleep, which is regarded as a "filler stage."

REM pressure   By using an EEG machine it is theoretically possible to deprive people of particular stages of sleep. In practice it is difficult because of the compensatory systems in the brain. REM sleep deprivation involves waking someone up whenever he or she goes into REM. In the first cycle of sleep this is quite easy as it is of fairly short duration (about 10–15 minutes). The second cycle normally consists of more REM sleep and again, this is relatively easy to disrupt. It is much more difficult in the third cycle as the brain is already trying to compensate for the REM that has been lost in the first two cycles. The ultradian rhythm is disturbed and REM starts sooner. If this REM is disrupted, then the fourth cycle REM starts sooner still and similarly the fifth. By the second night of deprivation there is a lot of REM trying to get in and so the night generally becomes very disrupted. This demand for REM is known as REM pressure.

There is a similar and stronger demand for deep sleep. In fact, to deprive a person of deep sleep soon means total deprivation, because the demand for deep sleep becomes so intense that the subject has to be continually woken up to prevent him or her from going into deep sleep.

When I come to sleep problems later on in the book, I will be elaborating on what is basically a simple model of sleep, illustrated below. There is a division between mental and biological mechanisms, with only emotions cutting across

A simple model of sleep

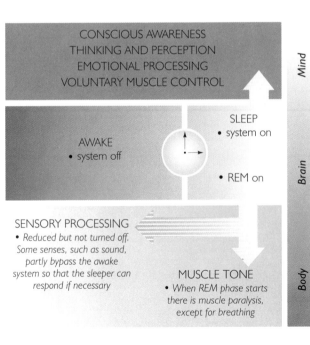

When the sleep system is active, conscious awareness is inhibited, thus allowing the awake system to remain off. Muscle paralysis is induced as each REM phase begins, intensifying the general muscle relaxation that has already occurred during the other sleep stages.

29

boundaries. This model is there to act as a temporary summary. The bottom of the diagram shows that during REM sleep, when the sleep system is switched on and when the REM phase of sleep has started, there is an active paralysis of the body muscles (except for breathing). So the general muscle relaxation that takes place (in people without sleep problems) when sleep begins and in the non-REM stages of sleep is further intensified by an active mechanism that induces paralysis. This active state of paralysis is one of the parts that can go wrong in various sleep disorders, such as narcolepsy (*see pages 117 and 134*) and REM behavior disorder (*see page 147*). Most people have suffered from sleep paralysis—waking up and finding that they can't move for 10–30 seconds (*see page 147*). It can be a frightening experience, but it simply means that the brain hasn't woken up yet! It occurs more often in people suffering from jet lag or doing shift-work, and for some genetic reason, the Japanese seem to suffer more from this than Westerners.

Sleep and other bodily and mental functions

It is not surprising that sleep is associated with changes in many mental and bodily functions. A state that occupies about a third of everyone's lives is bound to have an impact. For example, sleep affects both the senses and the memory. Sleep dampens the sensitivity of the senses, but seems to improve memory by strengthening memory traces. The former effect promotes sleep, whereas the latter improves daytime memory function.

Breathing becomes more shallow during sleep, but in snoring and sleep apnea (breath-holding) breathing is so impaired that sleep becomes disturbed and sleepiness results the next day. The 90–minute sleep cycle rhythm (*see page 24*) can also be found in the digestive system, but only in fasting conditions. Again, the relationship exists, although the functional importance is not clear.

Development of human sleep

The box on page 31 illustrates in a general way how an individual's sleep develops. In babies, the ultradian rhythm is much shorter than in an adult, running at around 60 minutes. Their sleep is also much more distributed throughout the day in early life, but as the months and years go by, the sleep is consolidated into the night. Melatonin secretion from the pineal gland reaches a peak at the end of the first year of life.

The process of sleep is not rigid and unchangeable. The brain systems involved provide a foundation, but learning also contributes to how sleep develops. Mental states, intimately related to the brain, clearly exert an impact as well. An adult's sleep is a fusion of a large number of different factors—so many that it is surprising that more people don't suffer from sleep problems.

There is little agreement on what is the function of sleep, but this may be because the question is not particularly clear. What is the function of wakefulness? There are many possible answers for both states. To make matters worse, much of the research so far has concentrated on Western industrialized man, therefore much of the speculation has been extremely focused. Nevertheless, sleep appears to be a vital state—animal experiments and neurological disorders that produce total insomnia both show this. Total loss of sleep leads to death, caused by increased energy expenditure, decreasing weight and a loss of control of body temperature. Most insomniacs never experience this total, devastating loss of sleep.

There is no strong evidence that disturbed sleep by itself causes ill health, but there is no doubt that quality of life is reduced. Disturbed sleep reduces the pain threshold, making pain less tolerable. People become irritable and concentration is reduced. The loss of control may aggravate or promote various mental illnesses. But is sleep good for you? It may not be. Death occurs most frequently around 09:00, particularly from heart attacks. The cause is not clear, but is thought to be associated with the increased load on the heart caused by getting up. Blood clots form more readily when your posture changes from lying down to standing up. On the other hand, Mark Twain did remark that beds were not a safe place to be, as so many people died in them!

Sleep development

Human sleep begins with sleep during the day and the night.

↓

A process of learning, conditioning, and training associates night-time with continuous sleep and daytime with continuous wakefulness.

To sum up

Chapter Three

Managing your sleep

Chapter One introduced the idea that three processes controlled sleep: the sleep system, the awake system and the biological clock. Sleep is not just a process of letting go, but two processes acting together: sleep taking over more and more of the brain, and the awake process decreasing its grip. The biological clock system appears to exert some control over the awake process. It can cause certain disorders when it runs at the wrong speed, making people go to bed later and later (adolescents and young adults are more prone), or earlier and earlier (older people have more problems with this). The clock also can run just slightly at the wrong pace, or the cues that synchronize it may not exert a strong enough effect. Cues include light, feeding, physical activity, work, and social activity. One reason why elderly people may go to bed progressively earlier and earlier is that they do not go outside enough, or get enough natural light from windows, to help keep their biological clocks set at the right time.

Early-morning person (lark) or late-evening person (owl)?

Some people prefer to work late, go to bed late and wake up late. These people are referred to as "owls." Others are just the opposite, preferring to get up early, start work early, and go to bed early. These people are called "larks." The questionnaire opposite helps you determine whether you are a morning person (lark) or an evening person (owl). You probably already know, but it is worth checking all the same, as the advice that relates to biological clock timing later on in the book needs to be considered in relation to which one you are.

Lark or owl?

Questions	YES	NO
Do you prefer to get up early in the morning (before 06:00)?		
Do you prefer to go to bed early (before 21:00)?		
Do you find it easy to go to bed at 21:00?		
Do you find it hard to stay up until 23:00?		
Do you usually become alert very quickly in the morning?		
Do you consider yourself a morning person?		

If you answered more than three of the questions yes then you could consider yourself a morning person. If you answered more than three of the questions no then you could consider yourself an evening person.

The ruler below illustrates the bedtimes and rise times that extreme larks and owls could have. There is no research to show whether owls and larks are likely to become partners or not! The important point is that if owls go to bed too soon relative to their clocks, they will spend a long time going to sleep. Also, if they have to get up between 06:00 and 08:00 in the morning, they will end up feeling they have not slept well enough or for long enough. They could well end up thinking that they were insomniacs.

There are distinct sleep patterns between larks (advanced sleep) and owls (delayed sleep). So if you have trouble sleeping, it may just be that you are not sleeping at the right time relative to your clock.

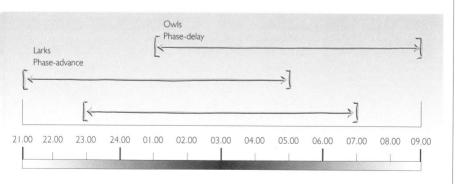

It is possible that body temperature curves run at different times in morning and evening types, as shown here.

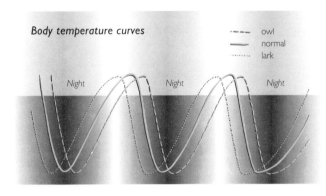

Body temperature curves
- - - - owl
——— normal
.... lark

Larks could try to force themselves to stay up later in the evenings, but are still likely to wake up early. Again, they too could misunderstand the situation and believe that they had a sleep problem.

The general population can appreciate the problems of extreme larks and owls, because movement across two or three time zones affects most people. When the clocks are changed in spring and autumn (daylight saving), many people have adjustment problems for several days later.

The illustration above shows the possible body temperature curves that morning and evening types may have. It is still not clear precisely how the clock system is affected: whether it runs particularly slowly in evening types and quickly in morning types, or whether it just runs at slightly different times in relation to light and dark.

Sleeping habits around the world

A study of sleep patterns around the world shows how sleep habits can adapt to different circumstances. In the developed countries, the transition from an agricultural to an industrial economy has caused many changes. The introduction of shift-work, the move towards an early-morning starting time for work, the development of the nuclear family unit, the separation of children from the parental or grandparental sleeping environment, and obesity have all contributed to considerable changes in sleep.

Yale University's Cross-cultural Survey (1937) noted the habits in siesta cultures throughout the world. In Patagonia:

"The Yahgans sleep together as a group and frequently interrupt each other's sleep ... a tired person will lie down for a nap anywhere and at any time." Comparisons of napping across siesta cultures show striking similarities: napping takes place mainly in the afternoon between 14:00 and 16:00; the length of the naps ranges between 1½ and 2 hours; nearly 90 percent of napping cultures are found at latitudes between 30° North and 30° South—the more tropical the climate, the greater likelihood that napping occurs. This is another example where temperature is involved with the control of sleep.

Towards the North and South Poles, daylight times become more extreme, increasing in summer until there is continuous light, and decreasing in winter until there is no sunlight at all. Not surprisingly, because of the effects of light on the biological clock, this has a major effect on sleep, and sleep-related disorders such as depression. A recent study in Svalbard, Norway—the most northern settlement in the world—examined how two ethnically different populations, native Norwegians and immigrant Russians, coped with the Arctic extremes of almost 3 months continuous daylight and over 2 months of complete darkness. Approximately 79 percent of the Russians had sleep problems, compared with 24 percent of the Norwegians. The Russians had more sleep problems during the polar night. Depression, dealing with shift-work, and inability to concentrate were common problems among both groups. Loneliness and alcohol consumption affected the Norwegians more than the Russians, who also noted worries as one of the causes of not sleeping well.

Daylight extremes

A circumpolar Siberian tribe, the Chukchi, were also observed from 1919–21 in a study by Yale University: "As the nights were growing lighter the irregular habits of the Chukchi became almost intolerable [because of] their complete disregard for all division of time ... One day they would sleep till noon, and would not crawl into their skins until midnight, get up, eat and go to sleep again in the morning. Day or night were ideas which no longer existed ...."

Sleeping environment Take a look at your sleeping environment, as there are various aspects that will have an effect on your sleep. The main factors are listed below.

Light Babies become infants, infants become children, and so on. During this time a strong association between darkness and sleep is learned. For some people this association is not important for sleep, but for others, whose sleep has become fragile, light is one of the factors that needs to be controlled. Thick curtains or effective blinds, or both, are worth considering seriously. Aluminium foil is a cheap, portable and temporary alternative. For those who have problems waking up in the morning, there are clocks with especially bright lights that strengthen the light of dawn.

Noise Hearing is actively reduced with the onset of sleep. Transmission of information from the ears to the auditory processing centers is reduced, but processing does not stop altogether. The brain's reaction to noise can be seen, when sleep is recorded using an EEG machine. Early research showed that the more salient and important the auditory information, the greater the brain's reaction—to the point that the person might wake up and be consciously aware of the noise. The noise of passing vehicles during sleep causes both a change in heart rate and a reaction in peripheral blood-vessels without necessarily awakening the sleeper or his being conscious of the noise. Nevertheless, the sleep is disturbed. A common observation among holiday-makers who go from a city environment to a quiet rural location is how much better they sleep, even if they are in different beds. Double- or triple-glazing is a general solution, although earplugs are a good alternative. There is an obvious danger with earplugs, however, that alarms may not be heard.

Noise is a problem in many hospitals, particularly in intensive care units, and it can be argued that the healing process would be helped if natural sleep were promoted. Research has shown that in neonatal intensive care units, babies with a very low birth weight sleep more deeply and cry less if "quiet hours" are introduced. The implication is that their sleep-awake cycles and general physiological stability are increased if these measures are adopted.

Aircraft noise can definitely affect EEG, indicating lighter sleep. There is inconsistent evidence of other effects: higher psychiatric hospital admission rates, visits to doctors, self-reported health problems, and use of medications. House insulation would help reduce noise, but not necessarily vibration. Mattresses will absorb vertical vibrations, but, depending on type, they may amplify as well as reduce horizontal vibrations. Even quiet traffic noise of 50dB, when accompanied by vibrations, is more disturbing than when there is just noise. REM sleep is more affected than other stages. Performance the following day can be impaired.

There have been attempts to make sleep more productive by learning something such as a foreign language, playing audio-tapes through specially adapted pillows. Unfortunately, the evidence suggests that it is only possible to learn material during the night if it wakes you up!

Safety

Many people complain that safety is a concern that prevents them from sleeping properly. This is difficult to deal with as sleep has probably evolved to allow for occasional checking of the environment, and this may be one of the reasons for the ultradian cycle (*see page* 26). Safety can refer to both physical and mental states. If the surroundings can be improved so as to provide a safer environment that in turn relaxes the individual, then sleep should improve. If safety of the psyche is the problem, then using the services of a cognitive psychotherapist would deal with this more directly. In the meantime, the thought-blocking exercises and mental relaxation exercises (*see page* 126) in this book could also be used. If safety has been an issue for some time, there is a possibility that conditioned insomnia has also developed (*see page* 132). Conditioning is enhanced with stress, the extreme seen in post-traumatic stress disorder.

Bedroom temperature

It is impossible to dictate the correct temperature, as this is a combination of the sleeper's own temperature, what the sleeper is wearing, bedclothes, and also the ambient temperature. Cooler temperatures are generally appropriate, but extremes should be avoided. Overheating may not only disturb sleep, possibly with adverse daytime consequences, but may also damage the skin.

Benjamin Franklin thought it was impossible to sleep when too hot, so he used two beds in a cold bedroom. When he found himself too hot in one bed, he would move to the other. Churchill, whose sleeping behavior was quite unusual anyway, also preferred to have two beds, but in his case he preferred sleeping in an unwrinkled bed so would move to a fresh bed when he had rumpled the first one!

Beds Getting the right bed and pillow is important for a good night's sleep. If you wake up with aches and pains that disappear without treatment in one or two hours then it might be the sleeping surface that is causing the problem.

Ideally, mattresses should make uninterrupted contact and distribute pressure evenly across the body. Hard mattresses have limited contact points, usually bottom and shoulders, so that pressure may lead to numbing and pain. Soft mattresses provide continual body contact but the neck and spine can sag, causing muscle tension and pain in some individuals (if you can sleep in a hammock or on a water mattress then a soft mattress will not trouble you).

According to a German proverb: *The best pillow is a clear conscience*. Pillows should support your neck as well as your head. This is achieved by filling the space between neck and mattress, maintaining a straight line between the neck and spine. A specially designed posture support pillow may achieve this. It is helpful if hypoallergenic material is used for pillows and mattresses, as runny and stuffy noses or asthma can disturb sleep sufficiently to cause daytime performance problems. In schoolchildren this could manifest itself either as poor school performance or poor behavior.

Sleeping posture It is possible to fall asleep in many positions, but some may lead to aches and pains. Your spine is aligned when you sleep on your side or back, but it is twisted if you sleep on your stomach, perhaps with one leg drawn up, bent at the knee. Misalignment may eventually occur leading to muscle tension and pain. There are various patented pillows with built-in head and neck support that claim to keep your spine aligned. If in doubt, consult a chiropractor or osteopath. Bed alignment was considered appropriate by the author Charles Dickens. He carried a compass on his journeys so that he could align his bed north to south—he thought that the flow of magnetic current would benefit the sleeper.

Sleeping together

It is not unusual to find people sleeping in all kinds of places and in all sorts of positions, either alone, as couples or in groups. As long as the situation is not dangerous, and as long as you wake up feeling OK, are not stiff and do not fall asleep involuntarily during the day, then there is nothing to worry about.

In the West, the double bed is almost universal, and it is regarded as normal for couples to sleep together. However, this has not necessarily always been the case, as this quotation from Dr. James Graham in 1775 shows:

> There is not in my opinion anything in nature which is more immediately calculated totally to subject health, strength, love, esteem, and indeed everything that is desirable in the married state, than that odious, most indelicate, and most hurtful custom of man and wife continually pigging together, in one and the same bed. Nothing more unwise—nothing more indecent—nothing more unnatural, than for a man and a woman to sleep, and snore, and steam, and do everything else that's indelicate together, three hundred and sixty-five times—every year.

Sleeping together is simply variable, and depends a great deal on the culture. American children sleeping in the same bed would be regarded as unusual, and most would find it desirable to sleep in their own bed, in their own bedroom. In contrast, Polynesian children would consider themselves abused if they were forced to sleep in this way because sleeping together as a group is still the normal practice in their society.

Bedtime routines Regularity in routine is the rule for good sleep. Every night the biological clock is resynchronized to the sleep-awake routine. Even minor changes in routine can have a negative effect on this synchronization. It is a common experience to lie in at weekends, and then find it difficult to go back to school or work on the Monday. Assuming nothing else was done over the weekend to disturb sleep, the probable cause is the desynchronization between the biological clock and the sleep-awake cycle.

Bearing in mind that light exposure in the evening tends to slow down the biological clock, and light exposure in the morning tends to speed it up, an extended time in bed in the morning will reduce the normal speeding up of the clock and thus delay the rhythm. This, coupled with the reduced time spent awake before trying to sleep, will lead to reduced sleep pressure and trying to sleep at a time when the biological clock will still be set for remaining awake. Even if you fall asleep, the clock will allow you to sleep longer the following morning, so when the alarm goes off you will find that you are sleepier than usual.

Menarche, menstruation, pregnancy and menopause Virtually every survey conducted shows that women suffer from disturbed sleep more than men. It is not clear why, but the changes in hormonal status when periodic menstruation first begins (menarche), during the menstrual cycle, and finally when menstruation ends (menopause) may contribute to this disparity. Other differences that arise from childcare, such as breast-feeding and the distribution of parental workload, may provide a background of sleep disturbance that eventually manifests itself as a long-term problem.

Certainly not all women of reproductive age suffer from severe sleep difficulties, but many experience some change. Women who do not suffer from premenstrual syndrome symptoms can still take longer to fall asleep, wake more often, and feel less refreshed after sleep during the luteal phase of the cycle. Sleep laboratory studies show subtle changes in sleep even in women who do not have any subjective awareness of any change. These changes involve an increase in the number of sleep spindles (patterns on the EEG) which peak during the luteal phase. The changes occur in parallel to the changes in core body temperature.

The "rhythm method" of fertility control uses body temperature as one of its guiding factors, and temperature affects sleep. This method can be very effective, but the change in temperature at the time of ovulation is similar in magnitude to the daily variation in most women. This makes it essential to measure temperature at the same time daily. Women who cross time zones or who are shift-workers may not only find difficulties in identifying accurately the time of ovulation, but their sleep may also be disturbed.

In pregnancy there are obvious changes in body weight and shape. In addition, in the third trimester the increased load on the heart and vascular system can lead to an increase in urine output that invariably disturbs sleep. There are huge hormonal changes during pregnancy, all of which have varying effects on sleep. In the first trimester, the feeling of fatigue may be caused in part by these hormonal changes.

Diet and drugs

Being overweight often causes problems with breathing which may disturb sleep. The disturbance may not be great, but is probably sufficient to disrupt sleep, and cause day-time sleepiness.

The hormones insulin and cholecystokinin are released in the bloodstream after eating. The insulin causes a fall in blood-sugar levels which probably brings about feelings of tiredness. Cholecystokinin has a direct effect on the brain, promoting a feeling of satiation and sleepiness. For night-time sleep there is evidence that eating small amounts of light food shortly before going to bed may make some people feel comfortably full and help them go to sleep. Obviously, it is particularly important that the food is easily digested—anything that is heavy or likely to cause indigestion is not going to help. Fewer calories are burned up while you are asleep, so weight-watchers should not eat before going to bed, whereas those who want to put on weight could.

Caffeine   Caffeine increases alertness and undoubtedly disturbs sleep. Differences in metabolism, even differences with age, all create considerable variability in how caffeine will affect an individual. What is surprising is how many people are addicted to caffeine. Try stopping for a day—if you end up with a headache and feel sleepy, you are addicted!

This naturally occurring substance can be found in the leaves and seeds of more than sixty plants worldwide, the most common sources being coffee and cocoa beans, cola nuts and tea leaves. It is added to many foodstuffs and drinks, so it is not just consumption of tea and coffee that should be watched (*see opposite*).

Caffeine is readily absorbed and peak concentrations occur in young adults 30–60 minutes after eating or drinking it (but illness or age widens the range to 15–120 minutes). It stays in the bloodstream for several hours, its concentration being reduced by half 3–5 hours after intake. Caffeine levels in the brain parallel that in the bloodstream, but if high doses are taken it may remain in the brain for 9–15 hours. Children tend to metabolize caffeine more quickly, as do smokers. This tolerance to caffeine not only varies over life but also varies with use. It is easy to get the shakes after too much caffeine if you have not had any for a while.

It is a powerful stimulant, but extensive research has not linked moderate consumption with any health problems, such as cancer, heart disease, or infertility, nor does it appear to affect the development of the growing fetus. Nevertheless, it does show powerful effects on the brain.

The amount of caffeine in coffee depends on both the bean and the way it is prepared. Tanzanian Peaberry, Colombian and Indian Mysore beans have the highest percentage of caffeine; Mocha Mattari (Yemen) and Mexican Pluma Altura have the lowest.

Guaraná   Guaraná (*Paullinea cupana*) is a tropical plant, grown in the Amazon region, which produces a small red fruit with a high caffeine content. It is chewed, or dried and the powder dissolved in water. The urban Brazilian version is a popular soft drink—insomniacs beware!

Caffeine levels in food and drink

Foodstuffs	mg
chocolate, unsweetened (Bakers) 1oz (25g)	25
chocolate, sweet (Bakers) 1oz (25g)	8
Jello 1oz (25g)	1–3
chocolate fudge mousse (Jello) 3oz	12
2 tablespoons chocolate syrup	5
3 heaped teaspoons chocolate powder mix	8
Dietary formula: 8oz (250g) Ensure Plus, choc (Ross Labs)	10

Soft drink	mg/12oz can	Soft drink	mg/12oz can
Jolt	100	Shasta Cherry Cola	44
Mountain Dew (US)	55	RC Cola	36
Diet Mountain Dew	55	Diet RC	36
Mello Yellow	51	Pepsi	38
Surge	46	Diet Pepsi	35
Coca-Cola	44	Canada Dry Cola	30
Diet Coca-Cola	40	Canada Dry Diet Cola	1
Dr. Pepper	40	Mr Pibb	41
7 Up	0	Sugar-free Mr. Pibb	59

Tea/coffee	mg/7oz cup	Tea/coffee	mg/7oz cup
Percolated coffee	115–175	Tea, iced (12oz)	70
Espresso (1½–2oz)	100	Tea, brewed 1 min	25
Brewed coffee	80–135	Tea, brewed 5 mins	50
Instant coffee	65–100	Tea, instant	30

Factors affecting caffeine metabolism

- **Exercise:** Moderate exercise increases the blood levels of caffeine, but also speeds up its metabolism.

- **Heredity:** Caffeine metabolism is controlled by many genes and racial differences exist.

- **Pregnancy:** In late pregnancy caffeine remains two and a half to seven times longer in the bloodstream. There are no placental barriers to caffeine, so the fetus is exposed to its effects. In pre-term infants caffeine is cleared out of the blood only very slowly.

- **Disease:** Liver disease decreases caffeine metabolism.

Substances that reduce metabolism and clearance:
- Grapefruit juice (not other citrus fruits; this is specific to grapefruit)
- Oral contraceptives
- Cimetidine
- Disulfiram
- Alcohol
- Idrocilamide

Substances that increase metabolism and clearance:
- Smoking/enzyme inducers
- Rifamprin

Alcohol In small doses alcohol can reduce anxiety and promote sleep. It does not cause sleep—larger doses may lead to unconsciousness and death—but it may aid the onset. It is estimated that eleven million Americans (6 percent of the adult population) use alcohol to promote sleep. The rate of alcoholism in insomniacs is twice that of good sleepers, and 60 percent of alcoholics use alcohol as a sleep aid. There is evidence that a sleep disorder usually exists prior to the development of alcoholism. Consequently it has been estimated that 9–10 percent of alcoholism is a consequence of insomnia.

Alcohol impairs breathing and therefore often causes further breathing problems for patients suffering from sleep apnea (*see page 135*). Middle-aged males who snore and

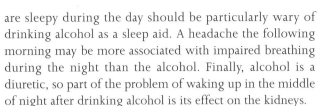

are sleepy during the day should be particularly wary of drinking alcohol as a sleep aid. A headache the following morning may be more associated with impaired breathing during the night than the alcohol. Finally, alcohol is a diuretic, so part of the problem of waking up in the middle of night after drinking alcohol is its effect on the kidneys.

Nicotine

Nicotine is addictive and causes respiratory difficulties. Both can lead to sleep disturbance. Withdrawal is associated with headaches and sleepiness as well as increased appetite and weight gain.

Marijuana

Tetrahyrdocannabinol is the active compound in marijuana. It may aid anxiety reduction and thus cause sleepiness indirectly. It takes longer to go to sleep after long-term use.

Cocaine and "crack"

Cocaine is a stimulant that produces euphoria. It works through the brain messenger (neurotransmitter) dopamine which is involved in the control of movement and wakefulness. Cocaine withdrawal is associated with sleepiness which may persuade the individual to take more in order to function properly.

Amphetamines ("speed")

Amphetamines are powerful stimulants that work by changing the level of several neurotransmitters including dopamine. Dopamine is altered in schizophrenia and this link is probably involved in the development of amphetamine psychosis. Amphetamine withdrawal is associated with increased sleepiness as well as increased REM during sleep. The increase in REM may be associated with nightmares.

Heroin

Heroin affects the pattern of sleep stages, but is most disturbing when it is discontinued. Intense nightmares may occur with the increase in REM found in withdrawal.

Sleep aids

Sleep aids that can be bought at pharmacies include pharmaceuticals, herbals, natural products and food supplements. Herbals, natural products (including melatonin), and food supplements are reviewed in Chapter Eight.

Over-the-counter aids

Pharmaceutical preparations generally contain sedating antihistamines, of which diphenhydramine is the most common. Diphenhydramine was developed to alleviate allergies, and the fact that it caused sleepiness was initially regarded as a side-effect. Subsequently, its use as an aid to sleep has become much more widespread although, unlike prescribed sleeping pills, high doses will not necessarily cause sleep. However, it has been used successfully as a sleep aid over many years without major incident or any major problems of dependence.

These sleep aids have two main problems: they take a long time to be cleared from the body and it is not obvious whether their effects dwindle over time. The directions on the label will usually tell the user to take these pills only at night-time and generally this should be OK (though some people may metabolize the pills slowly so should be careful that they are not impaired in the morning). However, in my experience many people also wake up in the middle of the night and take these pills. This is very ill-advised, as they are likely to impair their performance and cognitive abilities the following day.

Prescribed sleeping pills

Generally, the advice on taking sleeping pills to cope with life stresses is—don't. It is a definite *do not* if the stress is likely to be chronic and recurring. There is also doubt whether sleeping pills are useful for a stress such as bereavement, as there is evidence that it only delays the necessary bereavement process.

There are several types of sleeping pills available: barbiturates, benzodiazepines, and 'non-benzodiazepines benzodiazepines' (*see box right*). Barbiturates are very effective sleeping pills, as effective as a shotgun to the head—they are used as anaesthetics by veterinarians to put animals to sleep. Although effective as sleeping pills they are dangerous in overdose, particularly when used with other drugs, and provide one of life's sometimes revolving exit doors (Marilyn Monroe and Jimi Hendrix are two famous examples of celebrities who died as a result of misusing these drugs).

Drugs used as sleeping pills

• *Non-benzodiazepine benzodiazepines: Imidazopyridines and Cyclopyrrolones*
Short-acting, low daytime sedation risk, limited rebound risk.

• *Benzodiazepines*
All benzodiazepines have been associated with dependence after long-term high-dose use. National regulatory authorities almost invariably advise short-term use.

• *Chloral Derivatives*
May cause high dose-dependence. Risk of gastric irritation and overdose.

• *Barbiturates*
Risk of overdose, high dose-dependence, daytime sedation, biochemical tolerance.

• *Chlormethiazole*
Risk of high dose-dependence. Associated with nasal irritation and confusion.

• *Antihistamines*
Some toxicity in overdose, residual sedation. Can disturb normal sleep.

• *Antidepressants*
Some have a soporific effect. Older tricyclics are toxic in overdose. Invariably disturb normal sleep, especially serotonin re-uptake inhibitors.

• *Antipsychotics*
Risk of movement disorders makes antipsychotics, such as chlorpromazine, inappropriate for hypnotic use.

• *New drugs*
Some new medicines are on the horizon. These are either based on older remedies, or on some of the brain and body's own neuro-chemical control mechanisms.

Benzodiazepines are regarded as extremely safe in contrast to barbiturates as they do not stop respiration in overdose. However, they are not "pure" sleeping pills, as they

Drugs that affect sleep

Non-psychotropic drugs
Appetite suppressants • Antiemetic drugs • Antihistamines
Corticosteroids • Cardiovascular drugs • Hormones and Vitamin A

Psychotropic drugs
Tricyclic and tetracyclic antidepressants • Monoamine uptake
inhibitors • Monoamine oxidase inhibitors and reversible
monoamine oxidase inhibitors • Antipsychotics
Anticonvulsants • Hypnotics and stimulants

Recreational drugs
Nicotine • Alcohol • Caffeine • Herbs

Drugs of abuse
Cannabinoids • Hallucinogens • Anabolic steroids
Cocaine • Heroin • MDMA • Amphetamine

are also muscle relaxants, cause short-term amnesias and more usefully are anti-convulsants (anti-epileptic). Problems emerge with benzodiazepines primarily if they are used long-term. They invariably cause rebound (increased) wakefulness after short-term use. The "non-benzodiazepine benzodiazepines," such as zolpidem, are newer compounds that affect the same sites in the brain as the benzodiazepines, but are not in the same chemical class.

Research continues on identifying a "sovereign panacea" with close examination of the brain's own controlling mechanisms. In the meantime the field of sleep disorders medicine continues to advance, with more and more causes being identified. Treatments can become more specific as causes are discovered.

Lifestyle Unfortunately for all couch potatoes, moderate exercise has a beneficial effect on sleep. A recent study in the elderly (over 65s) found that exercise consisting of four 30–40 minute sessions of brisk walking a week was enough to improve sleep quality, the time it takes to go to sleep and sleep duration. Another study in a slightly depressed group aged between 60 and 84 examined the effects of a moder-ate weight-lifting program. These seniors engaged in their new exercises three times a week. Not only did their sleep improve over the 10-week period they were assessed, but also their depression lessened and other quality-of-life measures improved.

Early evening exercise may be helpful because it helps maintain general fitness, and the drop in body temperature after exercise may promote sleep.

As sleep is partly a conditioned process, any routine that is associated with going to bed to sleep is to be encouraged—putting the cat out, locking up, cleaning your teeth,and so on.

Pre-sleep rituals

Hot baths are often suggested and are worth thinking about. Baths have been advocated for their mental and physical relax-ation properties for many years, but the sleep researcher's perspective is different. It is thought that a bath causes a reactive decrease in body temperature which promotes sleep.

Hot baths

As mentioned before, alcoholic nightcaps are to be avoided, or the amount should be small. Surprisingly little research has been done on the effects of non-alcoholic bedtime drinks. In the 1930s two US researchers compared the effects on sleep of easily digestible snacks, such as corn-flakes and milk, with less digestible snacks. They found that sleep was less restless with the easily digestible snacks. At the same time Nathaniel Kleitman, one of the founders of modern sleep research, found that Ovaltine, whether made with water or milk, was associated with more restful sleep compared to other snacks.

A nightcap?

Since then, Horlicks has been examined at the sleep lab-oratory at Edinburgh University by Kirstine Adam. Initially, she found that Horlicks improved the sleep of middle-aged subjects but not young subjects. Subsequently, it emerged that subjects who habitually had a bedtime snack slept well after Horlicks or a nutritionally-equivalent meal, whereas subjects who did not usually have a snack slept best with-out anything. Habit is obviously important.

A cup of tea? Many elderly people have a cup of tea before going to bed or when they wake up in the middle of the night. The te will have an alerting effect, but if the ritual is part of the conditioned process of starting to sleep, and perhaps associated with anxiety reduction, it is quite likely that the alerting effect peaks after sleep has begun. As a night's sleep begins with deep sleep it may be quite a while before the waking up effect takes place. The same kind of pattern may also take place in the second half of the night.

Why can't I fall asleep? In the International Classification of Sleep Disorders (1990 there is a diagnosis of *Inadequate Sleep Hygiene*. This is defined as: "a sleep disorder due to the performance of daily living activities that are inconsistent with the maintenance of good quality sleep and full daytime alertness." Their list of diagnostics features is a useful guide to "inappropriate behavior." I have changed it into a list of "don'ts," with note on why each behavior is not conducive to good sleep

• Do not nap more than two times each week (lessens the need for nocturnal sleep).

• Do not get up or go to bed at irregular times (prevent the biological clock system from synchronizing with the awake system).

• Do not spend extended amounts of time in bed (if awake this causes inappropriate awake conditioning, if asleep i reduces the need for sleep the following night, and in some circumstances it can also reduce the cyclicity of the clock).

• Do not routinely use alcohol, tobacco or caffeine jus before bedtime (all of these can disrupt sleep).

• Do not take exercise too close to bedtime (this prepare the body for wakefulness, not sleep).

• Try to avoid exciting or emotionally upsetting activities too close to bedtime (they fire up the awake system, may induce muscle tension and prepare the body for action).

• Do not use bed for non-sleep (sex allowed) activities such as TV, reading, studying, or snacking (otherwise the bed and bedroom become associated, by a conditioning process, with wakefulness, not sleep).

• Do not sleep on an uncomfortable bed with a poor mat

tress, inadequate blankets, and so on (environmental conditions must be conducive to sleep, particularly if other problems with sleep are developing).

• Do not allow the bedroom to be too bright, stuffy, cluttered, hot, cold, or in some way non-conducive to sleep (the environment must be right; it should also be dark).

• Do not perform activities demanding high levels of concentration shortly before going to bed (they fire up the awake system).

• Do not use bed for mental activities such as thinking, planning or reminiscing (bed is for sleep, so do not condition yourself to remain awake).

Chapter Four

Lifestyle and sleep

Life's various demands—children, the ill, the incapacitated, work, even holidays—all eat into our waking time, with the result that sleep is often neglected. For many of us, this does not cause a problem. Our genetic constitution, our general health, the adaptability of our sleep-awake systems and how they interact with our internal biological clock, allow us to get sleep when we need it. But others are not so lucky.

For them, the biological clock is an important determinant of when they go to sleep and when they wake up, how alert they feel and how well they can do tasks. The biological clock's effect on alertness is much greater than is usually appreciated. It is not total, but a reasonable guestimate is that at least 50 percent of people rely heavily on the clock running correctly. Even a 1-hour change in time, say for daylight savings, has a measurable effect on the population as a whole.

This chapter will look at jet lag and shift-work first, because of the importance of appreciating the interactions between the sleep, awake, and clock systems. Learning how to cope with these situations is a good primer for working out how to cope with situations when you cannot control your own sleep, or when you are acting as a carer.

Light and the biological clock

Czeisler of the Harvard Medical School has conducted research for more than 20 years into the effects of light on circadian rhythms. He has found that intense artificial light can shift the circadian (24-hour) rhythms that are controlled by the biological clock. The intensity of the light (10,000 lux for the technically minded) is much brighter

than normal indoor light and is roughly equivalent to the amount of light needed to take a photograph with a cheap camera that does not have a flash. The effect is so powerful that Czeisler and Harvard have patented the use of light for medical purposes.

This is one of the most important discoveries in sleep research in the past 30 years. Before, it was not thought possible to change the timing of the clock rapidly. The diagram on pages 56 illustrates the effect. If you are exposed to light prior to your body temperature minimum (say in the evening) this tends to force the minimum away from its usual time. In other words, you will wake up later. Conversely, if light (usually dawn) is present short-ly after body temperature minimum, then the following night the minimum occurs earlier—you will fall asleep ear-lier. This discovery has a direct bearing on how to cope with jet lag.

Jet lag

Jet lag is a good example of how things go wrong with the biological clock. It is caused by moving to a new time zone faster than the body can adapt. It can cause various prob-lems, but consists mainly of difficulties with getting to sleep and staying asleep. This can be coupled with sleepi-ness during the day and stomach upsets. The severity of the problem varies with the number of time zones crossed and the direction. A flight of up to 3 hours westwards generally does not cause a problem. Eastwards, though, and the problems begin. Getting to sleep, waking up, feeling well, feeling alert—nothing is as easy as it was. Make it a transat-lantic or transpacific crossing (more than three time zones) and the problems really start to mount.

Jet lag can be sufficiently debilitating to cause problems with work or enjoying a holiday. Long plane trips can lead to dry, itching eyes, dry or runny noses, headaches, muscle cramps, and various other symptoms of general malaise, but these are not representative of true jet lag. They are the direct effect of the flight.

Generally, individuals suffering from sleep problems get little sympathy. Sleep is regarded as one of those facets of behavior that an individual can control at will. Jet lag, however, is a common problem experienced by many—and an ideal way for good sleepers to begin to appreciate how a chronically poor sleeper feels! The jet lagged individual knows, at least, that the problem is not permanent.

Coping with jet lag First, make sure that you take care of all the problems that may be caused by the flight itself:

• Use creams to keep your skin moist and your eyes and nose comfortable.

• If you are traveling low-budget economy, remember your eye-mask and earplugs.

• If you are tall, try to find out what plane you are likely to be flying on so that you can arrange a seat that gives you lots of leg room.

• Revise your favorite muscle-stretching exercises.

• If you find aeroplane seats uncomfortable, then buy a traveler's pillow or any other device that will help you maintain a comfortable posture.

• If you take medicines consult with your doctor to check whether your flight might cause a problem. Also find out how to handle the time-zone differences. Do you take an extra pill or one less?

• Do not take sleeping pills or buy over-the-counter sleep aids. Prescribed sleeping pills can be of short duration so theoretically could be used on a flight, but there are two main problems. First, if there was an emergency you might not be able to cope. Second, these pills cause amnesia: you can wake up under the influence, engage in activities, and go back to sleep again. When you wake up again you may not be able to recall what you have done (or what you agreed to) when you were awake!

• Over-the-counter sleep aids that contain antihistamines (*see page 46*) stay in the brain far too long to be useful. You may sleep during the flight, but you might not cope with immigration or customs afterwards.

• Try to move your sleep towards the destination time before you leave, particularly if you have an important meeting. If traveling eastwards go to bed and get up earlier each day for a few days before departure. Conversely, travelling westwards, you should try to move your sleep time later each day and get up later.

Diet

Try to adjust your diet so that eating is more closely timed to your destination time. A special diet has been advocated for many years by the US military. The diet involves alternating between fasting and feasting. The principle is to eat high-protein meals when you are trying to stay awake, and high-carbohydrate meals when you want to be sleepy. This diet is outlined below.

Before the flight

• 3 days before the flight start eating high-protein breakfasts and lunches and high-carbohydrate suppers.
• Avoid caffeine (*see page 42*) and other mild stimulants except for mid-afternoon.
• 2 days before the flight reduce calorie intake to around 800 calories by keeping meals light. Keep the same balance of high-protein breakfast and lunch, and high-carbohydrate supper. Do not eat any food after supper.
• The day before the flight eat as much as you want, but keep the food balance the same, and don't eat anything after supper.

The day of the flight

• This is similar to day 2 and is a low-calorie-intake day (800 calories). Maintain the same diet as before. On the flight, drink lots of water to combat dehydration. Remember alcohol promotes dehydration, but as you are airborne you only need to drink a little of it! Even moderate dehydration can cause fatigue and listlessness.
• Set your watch to the destination time and just note how the airlines feed you at peculiar times.

After the flight (breakfast at your destination)

• Using destination time, get up half an hour before breakfast, and do some light stretching exercises. Drink one to two cups of strong coffee between 06:00 and 07:30. Today feast on a high-protein breakfast and lunch and high-carbohydrate supper. Avoid caffeine after breakfast and no naps during the day. Keep as active as possible.

Finding light and avoiding light

The beginning of this chapter focused on the effects of light on the biological clock. You can use this to speed up your adjustment to a new time zone. The important factor is how much light reaches your eyes. You can sit in the shade outside provided your eyes are getting the benefit of light. Sitting inside looking out of a window is fine. Generally, 2 or 3 hours difference eastward or westward causes few problems. Problems start from 4 hours onwards.

The most general advice to give when traveling east is that you should improve your adjustment by being outside in the morning and midday light. Traveling westwards, the middle and late afternoon light can help.

Two more examples may help. First, decide whether you are an owl or a lark (*see page* 32). If you are neither, and regularly get up at around 07:00 at home, you can assume that your body temperature minimum occurs around 04:00. Remember always to adjust your watch to the new time as soon as possible.

When you are traveling you can use light to help your biological clock adjust more quickly to your new time zone.

If you are traveling four time zones eastwards, then avoid light between 03:30 and 08:30 and then look for bright light until 11:30. If you travel four time zones west-

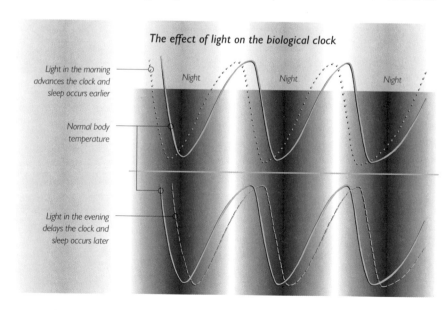

The effect of light on the biological clock

Light in the morning advances the clock and sleep occurs earlier

Normal body temperature

Night

Night

Night

Light in the evening delays the clock and sleep occurs later

wards, you should look for bright light between 21:30 and 00:30, and then avoid bright light until 04:30 or later. Clearly, westwards is a problem unless you are staying at a hotel that can provide special bright lights (*see "Sleep-tight rooms" below*).

These times need to be adjusted depending on your habitual wake-up time (and therefore your biological clock minimum). If, for example, you usually get up at 05:00, then the eastwards flight should be followed by avoidance of light between 01:30 and 06:30, and looking for bright light until 09.30. Similarly, a westward flight would be followed by looking for light between 19:30 and 22:30, and then avoiding light until 02:30.

"Sleep-tight" rooms

The Hilton hotel group has taken the problem of jet lag seriously. A number of its hotels boast "sleep-tight" rooms, which were specially designed with the National Sleep Foundation to help adjust to time-zone changes. These rooms have special light boxes and lighting systems, white-noise machines or soothing CDs, special mattresses and pillows, and earplugs. There is also a special two-call wake-up system for travelers who are not sleeping because they are worried that they might not wake up in time.

Shift-work

In 1991 the US Congress estimated that 60–90 percent of Americans on shift-work had sleep disorder problems. Shift-workers are static time-zone travelers. They have to optimize their working efficiency whatever shift they are on. There are no shift-systems that cater for the problems of biological clock and sleep-awake adjustment. Apart from accidents partly caused by working at night on shift (such as Chernobyl, Three-Mile Island, Exxon Valdez—all extremely costly accidents), shift systems do not appear to cause long-term health problems. But this may be illusory, as people who cannot tolerate shift systems leave their jobs. Vocational jobs such as nursing may end in failure because a person cannot adapt to working shifts. This self-selection reduces the possibility of detecting whether health problems are developing.

Nurses have often been studied on shift systems. More than 20 years ago, it was noted that nurses whose body temperature curves were beginning to adapt to their shift system were the ones who had less of a problem with shifts. The nurses whose biological clocks were difficult to change found shift systems more difficult. It was not known at that time that light could be a potent tool for changing the timing of the biological clock. This may also help others who have more difficulty in handling shift systems. Larks, and anyone aged over 50, seem to have more problems handling shifts.

Apart from trying to work at the wrong time relative to the biological clock, social and domestic commitments make life difficult for shift-workers. The work environment often does not have extra bright lights for the night-shift worker, and even going home after the night-shift means that light is re-synchronizing the clock to the wrong time. Once home, bedrooms are probably not adequately shielded, and rooms may not be sufficiently sound-proofed. Double or triple glazing, double blinds and thicker doors can all improve sleep continuity and quality by increasing the efficiency of the sleep system.

Dark goggles Bright light can be effective in experimental conditions in delaying the biological clock and improving sleep. So, potentially, it can be useful for night-shift workers. One study has found that bright light in the workplace (up to around 04:00) can help delay the sleep-awake cycle, but the journey home from work in the dawn light (in other words, after the temperature minimum) is enough to reduce its effectiveness. The solution appears to be to use dark goggles, which are darker than normal sun-glasses. Blinds, possibly double blinds, to prevent light getting into the bedroom are also extremely important for the shift-worker trying to sleep.

It has been estimated that out of all the cues that might align the biological clock with the sleep-awake cycle (food, social cues, noisy children, and so on), light might account for 70–90 percent of the alignment signal.

The answer varies depending on the shift-work scheme that you are on, what type of person you are on the lark/owl continuum, how old you are, and what kind of sleeper you are. You need to identify these features in the various question and diary sections in this book.

What should you do?

Astronauts are put on a 24-hour day-night, awake-sleep cycle, but NASA in the last few years has gone further in trying to improve the performance of its workforce. It has recognized that the best shift-work schedules involve long-term adaptation and that this is impractical. Using natural cues can also be impractical. They have found that self-administered light of 10,000 lux at appropriate times of day phase-delayed circadian rhythms sufficiently to allow the workforce to parallel the activity demanded by the Space Shuttle missions. NASA subjects not only reported improved sleep and performance, but better physical and emotional well-being as well.

NASA

Are adolescents and young people going to bed later and later? Survey results appear to indicate that this is the case. The ubiquitous presence of caffeine (*see page* 43) and many social factors will be helping young people to stay up, but once they do, the biology of the sleep, awake and clock systems will conspire to make them sleepy and alert at the wrong times.

The brain's biological clock generally runs slowly, and light towards the end of the day tends to slow it down even further. The melatonin secreted by the pineal gland will advance the clock, as will the dawn and morning light. However, if the youngster goes to bed late, the amount of time during which melatonin is secreted decreases (so the clock is advanced less) and they miss the early light (so again the clock is advanced less).

The upshot is that the clock remains delayed, so the youngster tends to go to sleep even later the following night. School or job demands will force them to get up the next morning, partially sleep-deprived and effectively jet lagged.

Adolescents

The elderly

The rulers below show typical diaries for the elderly. The top one shows an early night but early morning awakening. The lower one shows an even earlier bedtime.

Napping increases as a person gets older. This may be due to a number of factors: changes in lifestyle; the development of sleep disorders that disturb sleep during the night and increase sleepiness during the day; because an intrinsic rhythm of the biological clock re-asserts itself or the biological clock itself is running differently; or because various ailments of the elderly are disturbing their sleep.

Generally, napping should not be considered a problem especially if the individual does not regard it as such. Note the sleep taken over a 24-hour period and count the nap as

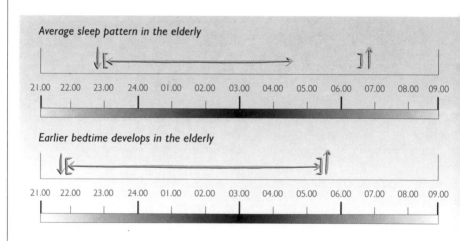

Average sleep pattern in the elderly

21.00 22.00 23.00 24.00 01.00 02.00 03.00 04.00 05.00 06.00 07.00 08.00 09.00

Earlier bedtime develops in the elderly

21.00 22.00 23.00 24.00 01.00 02.00 03.00 04.00 05.00 06.00 07.00 08.00 09.00

The earlier bedtime is also associated with daytime napping, as shown below.

part of the total. If this equates to an amount similar to that when you were young, then there is probably no problem. If you were a 6-hour sleeper, and you take a 1-hour nap during the day, then expect only 5 hours sleep during the night. There may be a problem if the sleepiness during the

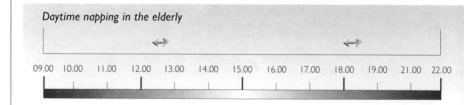

Daytime napping in the elderly

09.00 10.00 11.00 12.00 13.00 14.00 15.00 16.00 17.00 18.00 19.00 21.00 22.00

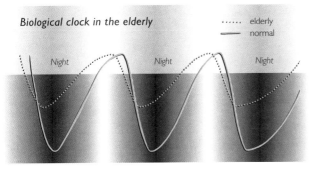

Biological clock in the elderly

...... elderly
—— normal

Night   Night   Night

The elderly tend not to go out as much, meaning that the effects of light on the biological clock are reduced. Sleep is therefore not as deep, more easily disturbed, and length of sleep is shorter.

day is uncontrollable (*see page* 134) and particularly if the night's sleep is considered unrefreshing.

The diagram above illustrates one of the problems that the elderly may have if they no longer go out much. Many elderly people go to bed earlier and wake up earlier, which may reflect a slight change in their biological clock time. If they also do not go out as much, it means that the synchronizing effects of light on the biological clock are reduced. This means that amplitude—the measure from peak to trough—is also reduced. This reduction in amplitude coupled with a slight drift to higher overall average means that sleep will not be as deep, will finish earlier and will be more prone to upset. The solution is to try to use ambient light, if not the specialist bright lights used by NASA, to enhance the amplitude of the rhythm. Just going outside in the evening light, or sitting in front of a window may do— it will indirectly strengthen sleep.

Doctors and nurses are more likely to be involved in road accidents when driving home if they have been working for extended periods. If you abuse your sleep your subsequent alertness will also be abused. Nevertheless, emergencies, illness, staffing levels, and so on may demand that medical, nursing and auxiliary staff work long hours. How do they cope in these circumstances?

Being aware of the dangers of unintended sleepiness is a first step. Most people can overcome sleepiness for short periods of time. The dangers are associated with boring

When your work demands that you stay awake

and monotonous tasks, such as highway driving. Naps do provide a great benefit. The longer the nap the greater the benefit. Caffeine is also a remarkably good stimulant and will make people alert, even though they may not feel well

Core versus optional sleep

When I was looking at the effects of sleep on memory, I ran an experiment that allowed the volunteers varying durations of sleep with little control of the sleep stages. The study was EEG controlled, so subjects were woken up when a cycle of sleep had completed (this would be at peak alertness on the ultradian cycle shown on page 65). Surprisingly the stages of sleep were less important than the duration. The longer the subjects slept, the better their memory. Since then, Jim Horne (Loughborough, UK) has suggested that the first three or four cycles of sleep are essential to function properly (core sleep), and the rest is optional.

Rules for core sleep

This means that there are several ways of obtaining core sleep if a whole night's sleep cannot be achieved:
• If you can, get at least 5 hours.
• Anchor sleep.
• Charge your sleep batteries.
• Long naps.
• Ultra-short sleeps.

Anchor sleep

Two UK researchers started investigating anchor sleep in the early 1980s. They divided an 8-hour sleep period into two 4-hour periods and kept one of those 4-hour sleep periods at the same time every day. They found that the circadian rhythms quickly re-established themselves if a period of anchor sleep was maintained, and it didn't really matter when the other 4 hours of sleep occurred. The core-sleep quota could be managed by taking additional sleep at some other time during the day. For shift-workers, this can be helpful, as they can choose an anchor-sleep period that is more or less constant across all their shifts. The minimum quota of core sleep can be achieved by having an anchor sleep and getting a second sleep some time over a 24-hour period.

David Dinges in the US has been investigating prophylactic sleep—taking some extra sleep in advance of an anticipated period of sleep disruption. It is not clear yet whether this achieves a significant improvement in alertness during the period of sleep disruption, but it does appear to have some positive effects. Again, if the bottom diagram on page 65 is considered, a sleep (a nap) prior to normal sleep will reduce sleep pressure. If sleep pressure is reduced by a prophylactic nap, then alertness may benefit.

Charging your sleep batteries

In situations where sleep is being disturbed regularly and waking activity is taking priority, then any nap is probably better than none, and the longer the nap the better. If naps are difficult to get started, then some of the techniques in Chapter Six may be useful (*see page* 119).

Long naps

In situations where sleep has gone wrong, the emphasis is on how fragmented the sleep has become and what impact this has on daytime functioning. However, if a person is a normal sleeper, someone who would sleep normally if circumstances allowed, then sleep fragmentation seems less significant. Just getting the sleep is important. It is not clear what the minimum should be: it might be as little as 4–10 minutes, but it certainly seems in the order of 30–40 minutes, not 3–4 hours. There is also some evidence that very short naps may prevent the rare but serious problem of "freezing"—failing to respond in a serious situation instead of acting.

Ultra-short sleeps

There are certainly problems to be aware of if you are having ultra-short sleeps, sleep inertia being the most important. Sleep inertia is a period of impaired performance that lasts between 5 and 20 minutes after waking up. It is a reality—US Air Force crews are prohibited from napping when on immediate alert or standby because of this fact. The recommendation is that anyone who needs an alert mind immediately on waking up should not take naps. Those who can afford to take a little longer to wake up could use the simple expedient of washing the face with cold water.

Napping and nappers

The top diagram (*opposite*) illustrates a normal night's sleep. Looking at the peaks, slow-wave sleep can be seen to decrease during the night. Slow-wave sleep is sometimes regarded as an index of sleep pressure. The decline is not continuous but oscillates. The slow-wave sleep troughs are punctuated by the 90-minute ultradian cycle.

The bottom diagram illustrates what happens after one night's sleep deprivation. The slow-wave sleep peaks are much higher and the decrease during the night is more rapid. Sometimes the ultradian cycle is also distorted and the slow-wave sleep cycles lengthen. Daytime napping has the opposite effect and decreases the peaks of the slow-wave sleep cycle. Slow-wave sleep is driven very precisely by the amount of preceding wakefulness before sleep onset. If slow-wave sleep is an accurate index of sleep pressure it is obvious why sleep advisers always suggest that people should not nap during the day. Reduced sleep pressure means that the interrupting ultradian cycle is more likely to leave someone wide-awake when they wake up in the middle of the night than it would if overall sleep pressure was higher. On the other hand, if you are not worried about getting a continuous night's sleep, and get a reasonable quota over a 24-hour period, there is no problem.

Claudio Stampi, a sleep researcher, has identified a number of famous nappers: Winston Churchill, Leonardo da Vinci, Napoleon, Salvador Dali and Thomas Edison. He found that Leonardo da Vinci adopted a very unusual sleep-awake pattern. He would sleep for 15 minutes out of every 4 hours, giving a daily total of only 1½ hours! Stampi calculates that during da Vinci's 67 years he gained in effect almost an extra 20 years by adopting this unique pattern of sleep.

Carers

Babies, toddlers, the ill, and the ailing elderly may demand so much of your time that you cannot manage a whole night's sleep. What do you do? Don't give up—there are various strategies you can adopt, including taking care of your core sleep, mentioned earlier in this chapter (*see page 62*).

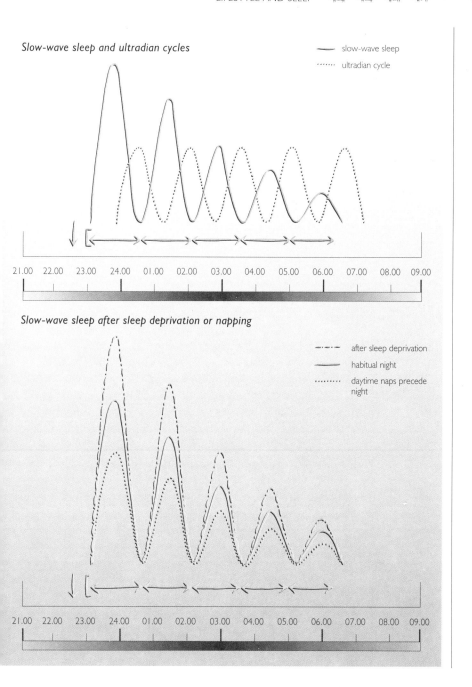

Slow-wave sleep and ultradian cycles

— slow-wave sleep
······· ultradian cycle

21.00 22.00 23.00 24.00 01.00 02.00 03.00 04.00 05.00 06.00 07.00 08.00 09.00

Slow-wave sleep after sleep deprivation or napping

–·–·– after sleep deprivation
——— habitual night
········ daytime naps precede
night

21.00 22.00 23.00 24.00 01.00 02.00 03.00 04.00 05.00 06.00 07.00 08.00 09.00

Self-help for carers Are you stressed by looking after someone else? The questions in the chart opposite provide an indication (tick the column that matches closest how you feel). If one or two ticks are in the "Nearly always true" column then you might start to look for help with caring, and help in taking care of yourself. In the meantime, the section called "Pulling it all together" (right) will try to help with your sleep, But first, some more sleep facts.

More sleep facts So far this book has talked about a sleep system, an awake system, a circadian (24-hour) clock system and an ultradian (90-minute) cycle. There are other ultradian cycles, and one of them runs every 12 hours. This became evident when volunteers were instructed to sleep for as long as possible. When they had slept around 12 hours the amount of slow-wave sleep started to increase (which didn't make a lot of sense as slow-wave sleep is promoted mainly by the duration of preceding wakefulness). This was evidence for a 12-hour cycle. Since then more evidence has emerged.

Peretz Lavie's 7/13-minute sleep-wake schedule has plotted what he called the sleep propensity function. The main feature is an increased ability to sleep during the night, but it also points to a 2-hour sleep cycle (possibly related to the 90-minute ultradian rhythm that has already been described) as well as an increased ability to sleep in the afternoon. He has also shown that there are specific, to use his term, "gateways" into sleep. These gates can also be closed, creating "forbidden zones." The forbidden zones occur in the evening prior to sleep, whereas the gateways exist just before sleep.

These observations explain why a nap in the early evening may not disturb sleep. The nap presumably takes place at the peak of the 2-hour cycle. If sleep is then attempted at the usual time, which should coincide with the main nocturnal gate, then sleep will run its usual course through the night (although awakening in the morning might be a little earlier). If the main nocturnal gate is missed, then the individual may find that they have to wait until the next gateway opens up.

Caregiver's stress test				
Questions	Seldom true	Sometimes true	Often true	Nearly always true
I find I can't get enough rest				
I don't have enough time for myself				
I feel guilty about my situation				
I don't get out much any more				
I have conflict with the person I care for				
I worry about having enough money to make ends meet				
I have conflict with other family members				
My own health is not good				
I cry every day				
I don't feel I have enough knowledge or experience to give care as well as I'd like				
I don't have time to be with other family members besides the person I care for				

Knowledge of the gateways and the cyclical nature of sleep is helpful for those who have problems with their sleep. Their anxiety about sleep can to some extent be reduced if they know that remaining awake in these circumstances is natural.

Chapter One described how sleep was an active process that interacted with the demands of wakefulness and various time-driven rhythms. This knowledge can be used to optimize your sleep time.

You may not manage to catch up with your sleep every day, but hang on and try to catch up with your sleep at least once a week. As the main stages of sleep compensate for

Pulling it all together

losses, one night in seven will allow you to catch up with a lot of the major sleep stages you have lost during the week. Staying in bed longer once a week can also help you recuperate without having an impact on your sleep in relation to the biological clock. You might be able to manage more than once a week, but if you start failing to sleep at your usual bedtime, then you should reconsider your strategy and limit the lie-in to once a week.

The recommendation not to nap (*see page* 64) is aimed primarily at those whose sleep is already failing and out of control; it is not directed at those who have to survive on minimal amounts of sleep. Along with other researchers, I argue that sleep is probably set up to occur mainly during the night, but not exclusively, with some time being allotted to it during the day. You don't have to listen to me— just talk to anyone who still lives in a siesta culture.

A study from the National Institute for Occupational Safety and Health found that naps significantly improve alertness, mood, and job performance. It also showed that the best, most refreshing time to doze is mid-afternoon, some time between 13:00 and 16:00, coinciding with many of the observations already noted in this book. How long you should nap for, you will have to discover yourself. As noted earlier, some people dislike naps because they feel awful afterwards. We know that these people run a slightly higher body temperature, but we don't know the most effective way of counteracting the negative effects (although they are likely to feel better later in the day). Sleep inertia is a problem, so be wary after a nap, don't make vital decisions and don't drive if you can avoid it.

Evening naps may pose a problem for night sleep, but on the other hand, if you are desperate to catch your favorite television program or remain conscious with your amorous partner, then an evening nap might be a lifesaver. Reading to children and then falling asleep for a short nap with them not only promotes a closer relationship but may also set you up for the night. Nap when the children nap. If they are cranky, but they do fall asleep in the car, take them out for a drive. When the children fall asleep, you might want to stop and try to get a nap yourself. (Always stop for a rest if you feel sleepy when driving, but remember—you may feel the effects of sleep inertia when you wake up.)

At work, a nap might be better than a coffee break if you can manage it. It partly depends what you need to do after the break. A nap may result in sleep inertia, but it will help you remain awake longer. Caffeine improves alertness very rapidly (within 20–30 minutes) and depending on your metabolism keeps you going for a couple of hours; but the downside is that you become dependent on it. If you think you need caffeine all the time, then you need to consider rescheduling your sleep another way. If you are a commuter, then take a nap on the train or bus, but use a travel pillow (or pocketbook, shopping bag, whatever) to support your head, and if you have a traveling companion get them to wake you up.

Alcohol is not a good idea. Use it as an occasional nightcap if you like, but be vigilant about how much you are drinking, and how often.

Exercise to maintain general fitness, but do not exercise close to bedtime. Once the body gets ready for action it tends to stay in that state for several hours. Do not be fooled if you fall asleep quickly after exercise; your sleep will be more disturbed and you will wake up less refreshed.

Finally, if your muscles are tense, and you suffer from headaches, stomach aches, anxiety, or depression, then you probably need to work on stress reduction. The fatigue may not be sleep-related, but stress-related.

Chapter Five

Using the diary

The diary and rulers are the most important part of the assessments, because they enable you to monitor your sleep accurately, so that you can start to work out what is going on. The daily questions and rating scale focus on some attributes and are used later in the assessment.

How to fill in the diary

The rulers were first introduced in Chapter Two to enable you to become familiar with them early on. I will now briefly recap on what they are and how to fill them in, and take you through the different sections of the diary to show you how to complete your diary pages.

Filling in the diary and rulers should not disrupt your sleep, and it is accepted that the readings may not be entirely accurate. You do not have to fill in the ruler during the night. And there is no need to stare at the bedroom clock. If you realize you are awake just mentally note the time and write it down in the morning. If you have to get up to attend to children, go to the lavatory, get a drink of water, or whatever, then also note the time.

The night ruler

A completed night ruler is shown opposite, with a reminder list of the activity abbreviations used. This night ruler illustrates quite a nasty night. The person goes to bed ($\downarrow$), then spends an hour reading. When he or she tries to sleep ($\lceil$), it takes an hour to fall asleep ($\leftarrow$), only to wake up 1½ hours later. About half an hour awake is followed by 3 hours of fragmented and troubled sleep ($\sim$). The sleeper then drifts off for 1½ hours of tranquil and pleasant sleep ($-$), only to wake up ($\rightarrow$) and spend another hour try-

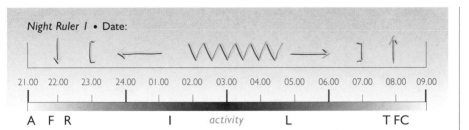

Night Ruler 1 • Date:

| 21.00 | 22.00 | 23.00 | 24.00 | 01.00 | 02.00 | 03.00 | 04.00 | 05.00 | 06.00 | 07.00 | 08.00 | 09.00 |

A F R   I   *activity*   L   T FC

ing to sleep again. The night ends with an hour of doing something such as watching TV ( ]) before getting up (↑). If this is you, you are probably in trouble; on the other hand, you may just have been on a long-haul flight!

Shown to the right is a list of abbreviations used to describe what you are doing during the night and day. The bad-night example is shown with these abbreviations included. The night starts (or finishes) with some alcohol (A) and food (F). The first period awake in bed is spent reading (R). Sleep is broken by some interruption (I)—this could be noise, such as a baby crying, or being too hot or cold, and so on. Later on in the night there is a visit to the lavatory (L) and the night ends by watching morning television (T). More detailed notes and observations can also be written on the page and in the box provided (*see "Notes and medication" overleaf*).

Activity	
A	Alcohol
C	Caffeine
F	Food
M	Medicine
S	Smoking
E	Exercise
D	Dreams
N	Nightmares
I	Interruption
L	Lavatory
P	Pain/Discomfort
W	Worries
T	Television/Radio
R	Reading

The rating scale

At the top of the next page you will see the rating scale. It will help you to identify how you slept during the night, and should be filled in within a few minutes of getting up. If you wake up feeling OK—neither tired and unrefreshed, nor really wide-awake or hyper—then put a cross on the scale below the "OK." If you are feeling really quite well and refreshed, then mark the scale a little higher, say 8 (*as shown*). On the other hand, if you are feeling only a little bit better than dead, mark the scale much lower, say 1 or 2!

If you have had a bad night's sleep, then you won't be surprised to note that you feel unrefreshed. On the other hand, disorders such as sleep apnea (*see page 135*) or periodic limb movement (*see page 140*) could be causing the problem.

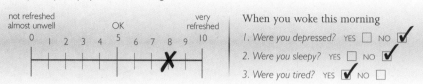

Complete promptly in the morning

When you woke this morning

1. Were you depressed? YES ☐ NO ☑
2. Were you sleepy? YES ☐ NO ☑
3. Were you tired? YES ☑ NO ☐

With these disorders your sleep can be disturbed without your being conscious of any disturbance (your partner may be able to shed some light here).

Daily questions There are also some questions that need to be completed in the morning, to help you assess the quality of your sleep. Here you have to decide how you feel, rather than putting a cross on a scale (*see above*). You need to decide, on balance, if you are depressed, or sleepy (wanting to go back to sleep), or tired (not sleeping but feeling that you should feel sleepy).

The day ruler You fill in the day ruler just as you would the night ruler, marking on the relevant activities in the activity panel (*see ruler below*). If you have a nap during the day, make sure you mark this on in the sleep area across the top of the ruler.

Notes and medication This section is to remind you of any events that might have affected your sleep—personal or work problems, for example—and also any medication that you may have taken.

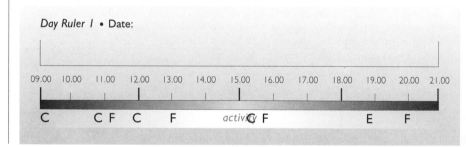

Day Ruler 1 • **Date:**

72

The Diary

You should now be able to complete the rulers and rating scale. You need to do this for two weeks—it takes this long to get a really good assessment of what is happening to your sleep. After 14 days, go to page 102 and complete the questions. You will then be able to assess your sleep and your general status. Chapter Six describes various routines and techniques that you can use to improve your sleep. In conjunction with these techniques you should then go back and complete the next two weeks of the diary. This will enable you to see if there is any improvement in your sleep. Try to fill in the diary for a typical month, not when you are on holiday, or abroad on business.

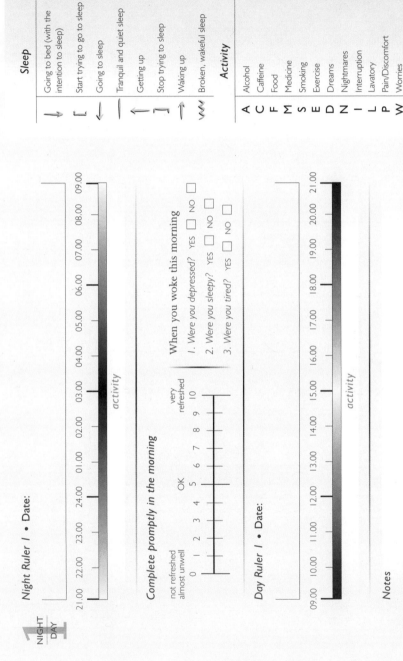

NIGHT
DAY

Night Ruler 1 • Date:

21.00 22.00 23.00 24.00 01.00 02.00 03.00 04.00 05.00 06.00 07.00 08.00 09.00

activity

Complete promptly in the morning

not refreshed
almost unwell   OK   very refreshed

0   1   2   3   4   5   6   7   8   9   10

When you woke this morning

1. Were you depressed?   YES ☐   NO ☐
2. Were you sleepy?   YES ☐   NO ☐
3. Were you tired?   YES ☐   NO ☐

Day Ruler 1 • Date:

09.00 10.00 11.00 12.00 13.00 14.00 15.00 16.00 17.00 18.00 19.00 20.00 21.00

activity

Notes

Medication

Sleep

↓	Going to bed (with the intention to sleep)
[	Start trying to go to sleep
↓	Going to sleep
|	Tranquil and quiet sleep
←	Getting up
]	Stop trying to sleep
↑	Waking up.
∿	Broken, wakeful sleep

Activity

A	Alcohol
C	Caffeine
F	Food
M	Medicine
S	Smoking
E	Exercise
D	Dreams
N	Nightmares
I	Interruption
L	Lavatory
P	Pain/Discomfort
W	Worries
T	Television/Radio
R	Reading

Night Ruler 2 • Date:

21.00 22.00 23.00 24.00 01.00 02.00 03.00 04.00 05.00 06.00 07.00 08.00 09.00

activity

Complete promptly in the morning

not refreshed
almost unwell   OK   very
refreshed

0   1   2   3   4   5   6   7   8   9   10

When you woke this morning

1. Were you depressed?   YES ☐   NO ☐
2. Were you sleepy?   YES ☐   NO ☐
3. Were you tired?   YES ☐   NO ☐

Day Ruler 2 • Date:

09.00 10.00 11.00 12.00 13.00 14.00 15.00 16.00 17.00 18.00 19.00 20.00 21.00

activity

Notes

Medication

Sleep

↓	Going to bed (with the intention to sleep)
[	Start trying to go to sleep
↙	Going to sleep
|	Tranquil and quiet sleep
↖	Getting up
⌐	Stop trying to sleep
↑	Waking up
∿∿	Broken, wakeful sleep

Activity

A   Alcohol
C   Caffeine
F   Food
M   Medicine
S   Smoking
E   Exercise
D   Dreams
N   Nightmares
I   Interruption
L   Lavatory
P   Pain/Discomfort
W   Worries
T   Television/Radio
R   Reading

NIGHT
DAY 2

![NIGHT DAY]

Night Ruler 3 • Date:

21.00 22.00 23.00 24.00 01.00 02.00 03.00 04.00 05.00 06.00 07.00 08.00 09.00

activity

Complete promptly in the morning

not refreshed
almost unwell   OK   very
                                         refreshed
0   1   2   3   4   5   6   7   8   9   10

When you woke this morning

1. *Were you depressed?* YES ☐ NO ☐

2. *Were you sleepy?* YES ☐ NO ☐

3. *Were you tired?* YES ☐ NO ☐

Day Ruler 3 • Date:

09.00 10.00 11.00 12.00 13.00 14.00 15.00 16.00 17.00 18.00 19.00 20.00 21.00

activity

Notes

Medication

Sleep

→	Going to bed (with the intention to sleep)
[	Start trying to go to sleep
↓	Going to sleep
│	Tranquil and quiet sleep
←	Getting up
]	Stop trying to sleep
↑	Waking up
∿∿∿	Broken, wakeful sleep

Activity

A	Alcohol
C	Caffeine
F	Food
M	Medicine
S	Smoking
E	Exercise
D	Dreams
N	Nightmares
I	Interruption
L	Lavatory
P	Pain/Discomfort
W	Worries
T	Television/Radio
R	Reading

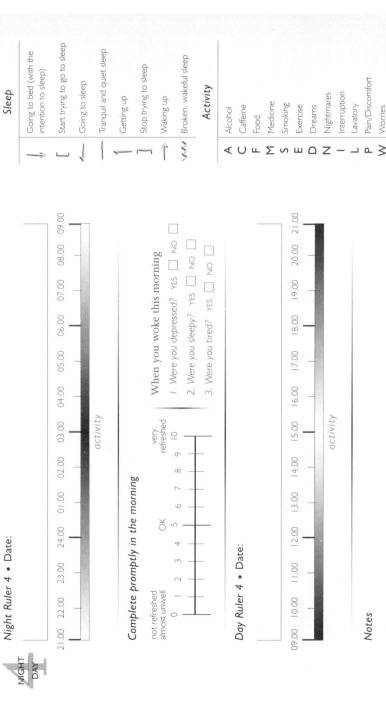

NIGHT / DAY

Night Ruler 4 • Date:

21.00 22.00 23.00 24.00 01.00 02.00 03.00 04.00 05.00 06.00 07.00 08.00 09.00

activity

Complete promptly in the morning

not refreshed
almost unwell

OK

very
refreshed

0 1 2 3 4 5 6 7 8 9 10

When you woke this morning

1. Were you depressed? YES ☐ NO ☐

2. Were you sleepy? YES ☐ NO ☐

3. Were you tired? YES ☐ NO ☐

Day Ruler 4 • Date:

09.00 10.00 11.00 12.00 13.00 14.00 15.00 16.00 17.00 18.00 19.00 20.00 21.00

activity

Notes

Medication

Sleep

↓	Going to bed (with the intention to sleep)
[	Start trying to go to sleep
✓	Going to sleep
		Tranquil and quiet sleep
←	Getting up
⌐	Stop trying to sleep
↑	Waking up
∿∿	Broken, wakeful sleep

Activity

A	Alcohol
C	Caffeine
F	Food
M	Medicine
S	Smoking
E	Exercise
D	Dreams
N	Nightmares
I	Interruption
L	Lavatory
P	Pain/Discomfort
W	Worries
T	Television/Radio
R	Reading

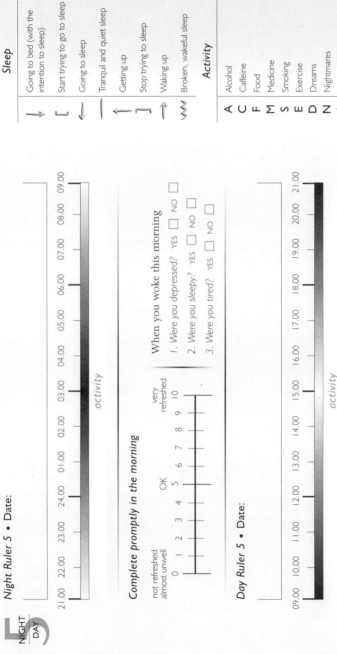

NIGHT DAY

Night Ruler 5 • Date:

21.00 22.00 23.00 24.00 01.00 02.00 03.00 04.00 05.00 06.00 07.00 08.00 09.00

activity

Complete promptly in the morning

not refreshed
almost unwell   OK   very refreshed

0   1   2   3   4   5   6   7   8   9   10

When you woke this morning

1. *Were you depressed?* YES ☐   NO ☐
2. *Were you sleepy?* YES ☐   NO ☐
3. *Were you tired?* YES ☐   NO ☐

Day Ruler 5 • Date:

09.00 10.00 11.00 12.00 13.00 14.00 15.00 16.00 17.00 18.00 19.00 20.00 21.00

activity

Notes

Medication

Sleep

↓	Going to bed (with the intention to sleep)
[	Start trying to go to sleep
↓	Going to sleep
|	Tranquil and quiet sleep
←	Getting up
]	Stop trying to sleep
↑	Waking up
∿	Broken, wakeful sleep

Activity

A	Alcohol
C	Caffeine
F	Food
M	Medicine
S	Smoking
E	Exercise
D	Dreams
N	Nightmares
I	Interruption
L	Lavatory
P	Pain/Discomfort
W	Worries
T	Television/Radio
R	Reading

Night Ruler 6 • Date:

21.00 22.00 23.00 24.00 01.00 02.00 03.00 04.00 05.00 06.00 07.00 08.00 09.00

activity

Complete promptly in the morning

not refreshed
almost unwell   OK   very refreshed

0   1   2   3   4   5   6   7   8   9   10

When you woke this morning

1. Were you depressed?   YES ☐   NO ☐
2. Were you sleepy?   YES ☐   NO ☐
3. Were you tired?   YES ☐   NO ☐

Day Ruler 6 • Date:

09.00 10.00 11.00 12.00 13.00 14.00 15.00 16.00 17.00 18.00 19.00 20.00 21.00

activity

Notes

Medication

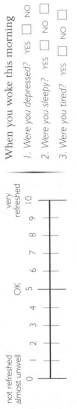

Sleep

↓	Going to bed (with the intention to sleep)
[	Start trying to go to sleep
√	Going to sleep
|	Tranquil and quiet sleep
←	Getting up
]	Stop trying to sleep
↑	Waking up
∿	Broken, wakeful sleep

Activity

A	Alcohol
C	Caffeine
F	Food
M	Medicine
S	Smoking
E	Exercise
D	Dreams
N	Nightmares
I	Interruption
L	Lavatory
P	Pain/Discomfort
W	Worries
T	Television/Radio
R	Reading

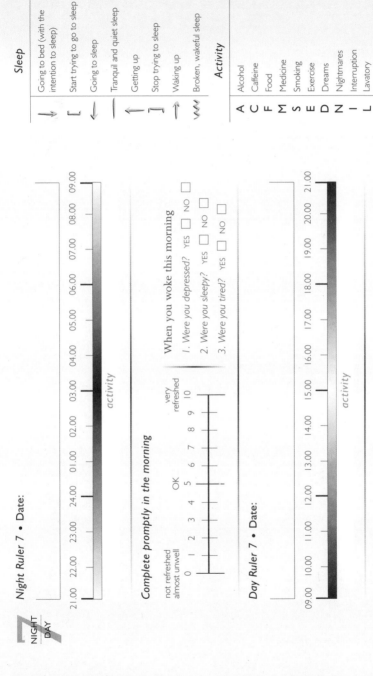

Night Ruler 7 • Date:

21.00 22.00 23.00 24.00 01.00 02.00 03.00 04.00 05.00 06.00 07.00 08.00 09.00

activity

Complete promptly in the morning

not refreshed
almost unwell   OK   very refreshed

0 1 2 3 4 5 6 7 8 9 10

When you woke this morning

1. Were you depressed?   YES ☐   NO ☐
2. Were you sleepy?   YES ☐   NO ☐
3. Were you tired?   YES ☐   NO ☐

Day Ruler 7 • Date:

09.00 10.00 11.00 12.00 13.00 14.00 15.00 16.00 17.00 18.00 19.00 20.00 21.00

activity

Notes

Medication

Sleep

↓	Going to bed (with the intention to sleep)
⌐	Start trying to go to sleep
↓	Going to sleep
│	Tranquil and quiet sleep
←	Getting up
⌐	Stop trying to sleep
↑	Waking up
∿	Broken, wakeful sleep

Activity

A	Alcohol
C	Caffeine
F	Food
M	Medicine
S	Smoking
E	Exercise
D	Dreams
N	Nightmares
I	Interruption
L	Lavatory
P	Pain/Discomfort
W	Worries
T	Television/Radio
R	Reading

NIGHT
DAY
7

NIGHT
DAY

Sleep

↓	Going to bed (with the intention to sleep)
[	Start trying to go to sleep
✓	Going to sleep
|	Tranquil and quiet sleep
←	Getting up
]	Stop trying to sleep
↑	Waking up
⋁⋁	Broken, wakeful sleep

Activity

A	Alcohol
C	Caffeine
F	Food
M	Medicine
S	Smoking
E	Exercise
D	Dreams
N	Nightmares
I	Interruption
L	Lavatory
P	Pain/Discomfort
W	Worries
T	Television/Radio
R	Reading

Night Ruler 8 • Date:

21.00 22.00 23.00 24.00 01.00 02.00 03.00 04.00 05.00 06.00 07.00 08.00 09.00

activity

Complete promptly in the morning

not refreshed
almost unwell   OK   very refreshed

0   1   2   3   4   5   6   7   8   9   10

When you woke this morning

1. Were you depressed?   YES ☐   NO ☐
2. Were you sleepy?   YES ☐   NO ☐
3. Were you tired?   YES ☐   NO ☐

Day Ruler 8 • Date:

09.00 10.00 11.00 12.00 13.00 14.00 15.00 16.00 17.00 18.00 19.00 20.00 21.00

activity

Notes

Medication

Sleep

→	Going to bed (with the intention to sleep)
[	Start trying to go to sleep
↓	Going to sleep
|	Tranquil and quiet sleep
←	Getting up
⌐	Stop trying to sleep
↑	Waking up
∿∿∿	Broken, wakeful sleep

Activity

A	Alcohol
C	Caffeine
F	Food
M	Medicine
S	Smoking
E	Exercise
D	Dreams
N	Nightmares
I	Interruption
L	Lavatory
P	Pain/Discomfort
W	Worries
T	Television/Radio
R	Reading

Night Ruler 9 • Date:

21.00 22.00 23.00 24.00 01.00 02.00 03.00 04.00 05.00 06.00 07.00 08.00 09.00

activity

Complete promptly in the morning

not refreshed
almost unwell   OK   very refreshed

0   1   2   3   4   5   6   7   8   9   10

When you woke this morning

1. Were you depressed?   YES ☐   NO ☐
2. Were you sleepy?   YES ☐   NO ☐
3. Were you tired?   YES ☐   NO ☐

Day Ruler 9 • Date:

09.00 10.00 11.00 12.00 13.00 14.00 15.00 16.00 17.00 18.00 19.00 20.00 21.00

activity

Notes

Medication

10

NIGHT
DAY

Night Ruler 10 • Date:

| 21.00 | 22.00 | 23.00 | 24.00 | 01.00 | 02.00 | 03.00 | 04.00 | 05.00 | 06.00 | 07.00 | 08.00 | 09.00 |

activity

Complete promptly in the morning

not refreshed
almost unwell   OK   very refreshed

| 0 | 1 | 2 | 3 | 4 | 5 | 6 | 7 | 8 | 9 | 10 |

When you woke this morning

1. Were you depressed? YES ☐ NO ☐
2. Were you sleepy? YES ☐ NO ☐
3. Were you tired? YES ☐ NO ☐

Day Ruler 10 • Date:

| 09.00 | 10.00 | 11.00 | 12.00 | 13.00 | 14.00 | 15.00 | 16.00 | 17.00 | 18.00 | 19.00 | 20.00 | 21.00 |

activity

Notes

Medication

Sleep

↓	Going to bed (with the intention to sleep)
[	Start trying to go to sleep
↓	Going to sleep
|	Tranquil and quiet sleep
←	Getting up
]	Stop trying to sleep
↑	Waking up
∿	Broken, wakeful sleep

Activity

A Alcohol
C Caffeine
F Food
M Medicine
S Smoking
E Exercise
D Dreams
N Nightmares
I Interruption
L Lavatory
P Pain/Discomfort
W Worries
T Television/Radio
R Reading

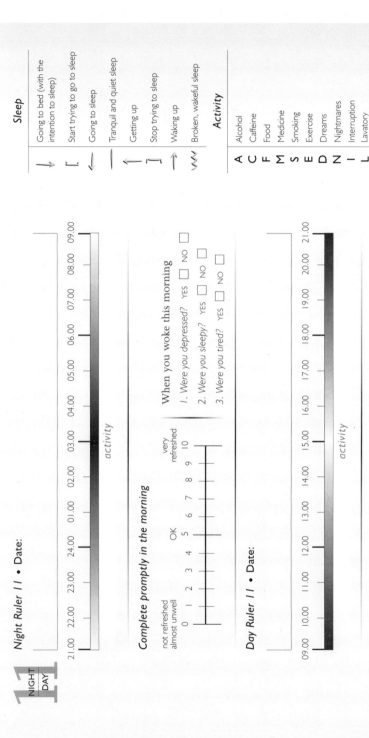

NIGHT
DAY
11

Night Ruler 11 • Date:

21.00 22.00 23.00 24.00 01.00 02.00 03.00 04.00 05.00 06.00 07.00 08.00 09.00

activity

Complete promptly in the morning

not refreshed
almost unwell   OK   very
                                          refreshed

0   1   2   3   4   5   6   7   8   9   10

When you woke this morning

1. *Were you depressed?* YES ☐ NO ☐
2. *Were you sleepy?* YES ☐ NO ☐
3. *Were you tired?* YES ☐ NO ☐

Day Ruler 11 • Date:

09.00 10.00 11.00 12.00 13.00 14.00 15.00 16.00 17.00 18.00 19.00 20.00 21.00

activity

Notes

Medication

Sleep

↘ Going to bed (with the intention to sleep)
[· Start trying to go to sleep
↓ Going to sleep
| Tranquil and quiet sleep
↙ Getting up
] Stop trying to sleep
↑ Waking up
∿ Broken, wakeful sleep

Activity

A Alcohol
C Caffeine
F Food
M Medicine
S Smoking
E Exercise
D Dreams
N Nightmares
I Interruption
L Lavatory
P Pain/Discomfort
W Worries
T Television/Radio
R Reading

12
NIGHT
DAY

Night Ruler 12 • Date:

21.00 22.00 23.00 24.00 01.00 02.00 03.00 04.00 05.00 06.00 07.00 08.00 09.00

activity

Complete promptly in the morning

not refreshed
almost unwell   OK   very refreshed

0 1 2 3 4 5 6 7 8 9 10

When you woke this morning

1. Were you depressed? YES ☐ NO ☐
2. Were you sleepy? YES ☐ NO ☐
3. Were you tired? YES ☐ NO ☐

Day Ruler 12 • Date:

09.00 10.00 11.00 12.00 13.00 14.00 15.00 16.00 17.00 18.00 19.00 20.00 21.00

activity

Notes

Medication

Sleep

↓	Going to bed (with the intention to sleep)
[	Start trying to go to sleep
✓	Going to sleep
|	Tranquil and quiet sleep
↰	Getting up
]	Stop trying to sleep
↑	Waking up
∨∨∨	Broken, wakeful sleep

Activity

A	Alcohol
C	Caffeine
F	Food
M	Medicine
S	Smoking
E	Exercise
D	Dreams
N	Nightmares
I	Interruption
L	Lavatory
P	Pain/Discomfort
W	Worries
T	Television/Radio
R	Reading

13 NIGHT DAY

Night Ruler 13 • Date:

21.00. 22.00 23.00 24.00 01.00 02.00 03.00 04.00 05.00 06.00 07.00 08.00 09.00

activity

Complete promptly in the morning

not refreshed
almost unwell
OK
very refreshed

0 1 2 3 4 5 6 7 8 9 10

When you woke this morning

1. Were you depressed? YES ☐ NO ☐
2. Were you sleepy? YES ☐ NO ☐
3. Were you tired? YES ☐ NO ☐

Day Ruler 13 • Date:

09.00 10.00 11.00 12.00 13.00 14.00 15.00 16.00 17.00 18.00 19.00 20.00 21.00

activity

Notes

Medication

Sleep

→   Going to bed (with the intention to sleep)
⌐   Start trying to go to sleep
↓   Going to sleep
| Tranquil and quiet sleep
←   Getting up
⌐   Stop trying to sleep
↑   Waking up
〰   Broken, wakeful sleep

Activity

A   Alcohol
C   Caffeine
F   Food
M   Medicine
S   Smoking
E   Exercise
D   Dreams
N   Nightmares
I   Interruption
L   Lavatory
P   Pain/Discomfort
W   Worries
T   Television/Radio
R   Reading

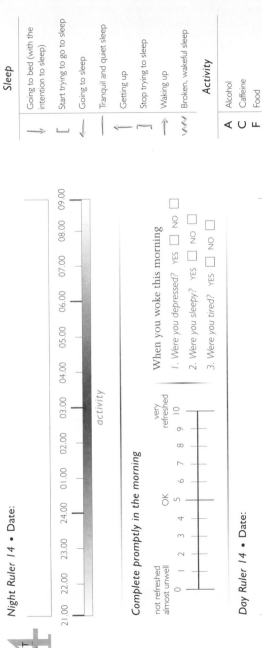

Night Ruler 14 • Date:

21.00 22.00 23.00 24.00 01.00 02.00 03.00 04.00 05.00 06.00 07.00 08.00 09.00

activity

Complete promptly in the morning

not refreshed
almost unwell   OK   very refreshed

0   1   2   3   4   5   6   7   8   9   10

When you woke this morning

1. *Were you depressed?*   YES ☐   NO ☐

2. *Were you sleepy?*   YES ☐   NO ☐

3. *Were you tired?*   YES ☐   NO ☐

Day Ruler 14 • Date:

09.00 10.00 11.00 12.00 13.00 14.00 15.00 16.00 17.00 18.00 19.00 20.00 21.00

activity

Notes

Medication

• *Now refer to page 73 to find out what to do next.*

Sleep

↓	Going to bed (with the intention to sleep)
[	Start trying to go to sleep
↓	Going to sleep
|	Tranquil and quiet sleep
←	Getting up
]	Stop trying to sleep
↑	Waking up
ϟϟ	Broken, wakeful sleep

Activity

A	Alcohol
C	Caffeine
F	Food
M	Medicine
S	Smoking
E	Exercise
D	Dreams
N	Nightmares
I	Interruption
L	Lavatory
P	Pain/Discomfort
W	Worries
T	Television/Radio
R	Reading

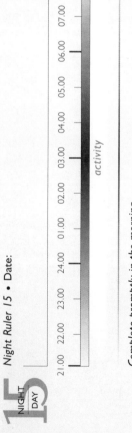

Night Ruler 15 • Date:

21.00 22.00 23.00 24.00 01.00 02.00 03.00 04.00 05.00 06.00 07.00 08.00 09.00

activity

Complete promptly in the morning

not refreshed
almost unwell   OK   very refreshed

0   1   2   3   4   5   6   7   8   9   10

When you woke this morning

1. *Were you depressed?*   YES ☐   NO ☐
2. *Were you sleepy?*   YES ☐   NO ☐
3. *Were you tired?*   YES ☐   NO ☐

Day Ruler 15 • Date:

09.00 10.00 11.00 12.00 13.00 14.00 15.00 16.00 17.00 18.00 19.00 20.00 21.00

activity

Notes

Medication

Sleep

→	Going to bed (with the intention to sleep)
[	Start trying to go to sleep
↓	Going to sleep
|	Tranquil and quiet sleep
←	Getting up
⌐	Stop trying to sleep
↑	Waking up
∿	Broken, wakeful sleep

Activity

A	Alcohol
C	Caffeine
F	Food
M	Medicine
S	Smoking
E	Exercise
D	Dreams
N	Nightmares
I	Interruption
L	Lavatory
P	Pain/Discomfort
W	Worries
T	Television/Radio
R	Reading

16
NIGHT
DAY

Night Ruler 16 • Date:

21.00 22.00 23.00 24.00 01.00 02.00 03.00 04.00 05.00 06.00 07.00 08.00 09.00

activity

Complete promptly in the morning

not refreshed
almost unwell   OK   very refreshed

0   1   2   3   4   5   6   7   8   9   10

When you woke this morning

1. *Were you depressed?* YES ☐ NO ☐
2. *Were you sleepy?* YES ☐ NO ☐
3. *Were you tired?* YES ☐ NO ☐

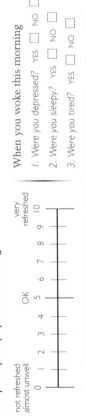

Day Ruler 16 • Date:

09.00 10.00 11.00 12.00 13.00 14.00 15.00 16.00 17.00 18.00 19.00 20.00 21.00

activity

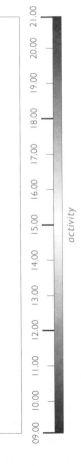

Notes

Medication

Sleep

↓	Going to bed (with the intention to sleep)
[.	Start trying to go to sleep
✓	Going to sleep
|	Tranquil and quiet sleep
⌐	Getting up
⌐	Stop trying to sleep
↑	Waking up
√√√	Broken, wakeful sleep

Activity

A	Alcohol
C	Caffeine
F	Food
M	Medicine
S	Smoking
E	Exercise
D	Dreams
N	Nightmares
I	Interruption
L	Lavatory
P	Pain/Discomfort
W	Worries
T	Television/Radio
R	Reading

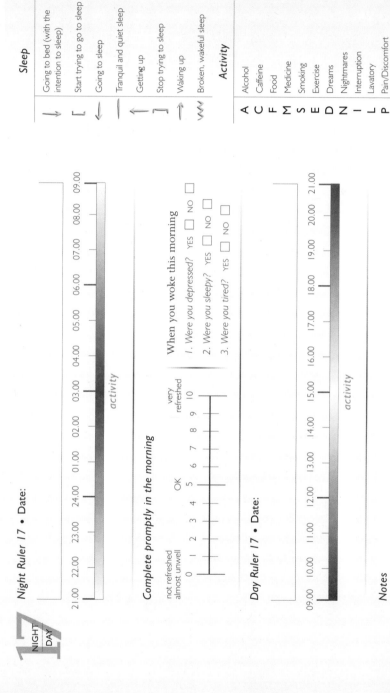

17
NIGHT
DAY

Night Ruler 17 • Date:

21.00 22.00 23.00 24.00 01.00 02.00 03.00 04.00 05.00 06.00 07.00 08.00 09.00

activity

Complete promptly in the morning

not refreshed
almost unwell

OK

very
refreshed

0 1 2 3 4 5 6 7 8 9 10

When you woke this morning

1. Were you depressed? YES ☐ NO ☐

2. Were you sleepy? YES ☐ NO ☐

3. Were you tired? YES ☐ NO ☐

Day Ruler 17 • Date:

09.00 10.00 11.00 12.00 13.00 14.00 15.00 16.00 17.00 18.00 19.00 20.00 21.00

activity

Notes

Medication

Sleep

→	Going to bed (with the intention to sleep)
[	Start trying to go to sleep
↓	Going to sleep
|	Tranquil and quiet sleep
←	Getting up
]	Stop trying to sleep
↑	Waking up
∿	Broken, wakeful sleep

Activity

A	Alcohol
C	Caffeine
F	Food
M	Medicine
S	Smoking
E	Exercise
D	Dreams
N	Nightmares
I	Interruption
L	Lavatory
P	Pain/Discomfort
W	Worries
T	Television/Radio
R	Reading

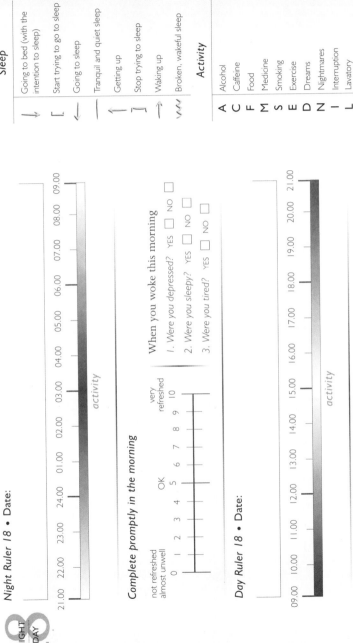

18 NIGHT / DAY

Night Ruler 18 • Date:

21.00 22.00 23.00 24.00 01.00 02.00 03.00 04.00 05.00 06.00 07.00 08.00 09.00

activity

Complete promptly in the morning

not refreshed
almost unwell

OK

very refreshed

0 1 2 3 4 5 6 7 8 9 10

When you woke this morning

1. Were you depressed? YES ☐ NO ☐
2. Were you sleepy? YES ☐ NO ☐
3. Were you tired? YES ☐ NO ☐

Day Ruler 18 • Date:

09.00 10.00 11.00 12.00 13.00 14.00 15.00 16.00 17.00 18.00 19.00 20.00 21.00

activity

Notes

Medication

Sleep

↓	Going to bed (with the intention to sleep)
[	Start trying to go to sleep
✓	Going to sleep
|	Tranquil and quiet sleep
←	Getting up
]	Stop trying to sleep
↑	Waking up
⌇⌇	Broken, wakeful sleep

Activity

A	Alcohol
C	Caffeine
F	Food
M	Medicine
S	Smoking
E	Exercise
D	Dreams
N	Nightmares
I	Interruption
L	Lavatory
P	Pain/Discomfort
W	Worries
T	Television/Radio
R	Reading

19 NIGHT / DAY

Night Ruler 19 • Date:

21.00 22.00 23.00 24.00 01.00 02.00 03.00 04.00 05.00 06.00 07.00 08.00 09.00

activity

Complete promptly in the morning

not refreshed
almost unwell   OK   very refreshed

0   1   2   3   4   5   6   7   8   9   10

When you woke this morning

1. Were you depressed?   YES ☐   NO ☐
2. Were you sleepy?   YES ☐   NO ☐
3. Were you tired?   YES ☐   NO ☐

Day Ruler 19 • Date:

09.00 10.00 11.00 12.00 13.00 14.00 15.00 16.00 17.00 18.00 19.00 20.00 21.00

activity

Notes

Medication

Sleep

↓	Going to bed (with the intention to sleep)
[	Start trying to go to sleep
↓	Going to sleep
|	Tranquil and quiet sleep
↖	Getting up
⌐	Stop trying to sleep
↑	Waking up
∿	Broken, wakeful sleep

Activity

A	Alcohol
C	Caffeine
F	Food
M	Medicine
S	Smoking
E	Exercise
D	Dreams
N	Nightmares
I	Interruption
L	Lavatory
P	Pain/Discomfort
W	Worries
T	Television/Radio
R	Reading

Night Ruler 20 • Date:

21.00 22.00 23.00 24.00 01.00 02.00 03.00 04.00 05.00 06.00 07.00 08.00 09.00

activity

Complete promptly in the morning

not refreshed
almost unwell

OK

very
refreshed

0   1   2   3   4   5   6   7   8   9   10

When you woke this morning

1. Were you depressed?   YES ☐   NO ☐
2. Were you sleepy?   YES ☐   NO ☐
3. Were you tired?   YES ☐   NO ☐

Day Ruler 20 • Date:

09.00 10.00 11.00 12.00 13.00 14.00 15.00 16.00 17.00 18.00 19.00 20.00 21.00

activity

Notes

Medication

Sleep

↓	Going to bed (with the intention to sleep)
[	Start trying to go to sleep
✓	Going to sleep
│	Tranquil and quiet sleep
⌐	Getting up
]	Stop trying to sleep
↑	Waking up
✓✓✓	Broken, wakeful sleep

Activity

A	Alcohol
C	Caffeine
F	Food
M	Medicine
S	Smoking
E	Exercise
D	Dreams
N	Nightmares
I	Interruption
L	Lavatory
P	Pain/Discomfort
W	Worries
T	Television/Radio
R	Reading

Sleep

→	Going to bed (with the intention to sleep)
[	Start trying to go to sleep
↓	Going to sleep
|	Tranquil and quiet sleep
←	Getting up
]	Stop trying to sleep
↑	Waking up
∿∿	Broken, wakeful sleep

Activity

A	Alcohol
C	Caffeine
F	Food
M	Medicine
S	Smoking
E	Exercise
D	Dreams
N	Nightmares
I	Interruption
L	Lavatory
P	Pain/Discomfort
W	Worries
T	Television/Radio
R	Reading

21 NIGHT / DAY

Night Ruler 21 • Date:

21.00   22.00   23.00   24.00   01.00   02.00   03.00   04.00   05.00   06.00   07.00   08.00   09.00

activity

Complete promptly in the morning

not refreshed
almost unwell   OK   very refreshed

0   1   2   3   4   5   6   7   8   9   10

When you woke this morning

1. Were you depressed?   YES ☐   NO ☐

2. Were you sleepy?   YES ☐   NO ☐

3. Were you tired?   YES ☐   NO ☐

Day Ruler 21 • Date:

09.00   10.00   11.00   12.00   13.00   14.00   15.00   16.00   17.00   18.00   19.00   20.00   21.00

activity

Notes

Medication

NIGHT 22 / DAY 22

Night Ruler 22 • Date:

21.00 22.00 23.00 24.00 01.00 02.00 03.00 04.00 05.00 06.00 07.00 08.00 09.00

activity

Complete promptly in the morning

not refreshed
almost unwell   OK   very refreshed

0   1   2   3   4   5   6   7   8   9   10

When you woke this morning

1. Were you *depressed?* YES ☐ NO ☐
2. Were you *sleepy?* YES ☐ NO ☐
3. Were you *tired?* YES ☐ NO ☐

Day Ruler 22 • Date:

09.00 10.00 11.00 12.00 13.00 14.00 15.00 16.00 17.00 18.00 19.00 20.00 21.00

activity

Notes

Medication

Sleep

↓ Going to bed (with the intention to sleep)

[Start trying to go to sleep

↙ Going to sleep

| Tranquil and quiet sleep

← Getting up

⌐ Stop trying to sleep

↑ Waking up

⌇ Broken, wakeful sleep

Activity

A Alcohol
C Caffeine
F Food
M Medicine
S Smoking
E Exercise
D Dreams
N Nightmares
I Interruption
L Lavatory
P Pain/Discomfort
W Worries
T Television/Radio
R Reading

23 NIGHT / DAY

Night Ruler 23 • Date:

21.00 22.00 23.00 24.00 01.00 02.00 03.00 04.00 05.00 06.00 07.00 08.00 09.00

activity

Complete promptly in the morning

not refreshed
almost unwell   OK   very refreshed

0   1   2   3   4   5   6   7   8   9   10

When you woke this morning

1. *Were you depressed?* YES ☐ NO ☐
2. *Were you sleepy?* YES ☐ NO ☐
3. *Were you tired?* YES ☐ NO ☐

Day Ruler 23 • Date:

09.00 10.00 11.00 12.00 13.00 14.00 15.00 16.00 17.00 18.00 19.00 20.00 21.00

activity

Notes

Medication

Sleep

↓ Going to bed (with the intention to sleep)

[Start trying to go to sleep

↓ Going to sleep

| Tranquil and quiet sleep

← Getting up

] Stop trying to sleep

↑ Waking up

∿ Broken, wakeful sleep

Activity

A Alcohol
C Caffeine
F Food
M Medicine
S Smoking
E Exercise
D Dreams
N Nightmares
I Interruption
L Lavatory
P Pain/Discomfort
W Worries
T Television/Radio
R Reading

24 NIGHT / DAY

Night Ruler 24 • Date:

21.00 22.00 23.00 24.00 01.00 02.00 03.00 04.00 05.00 06.00 07.00 08.00 09.00

activity

Complete promptly in the morning

not refreshed
almost unwell

OK

very
refreshed

0 1 2 3 4 5 6 7 8 9 10

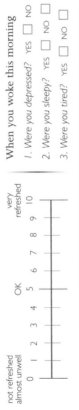

When you woke this morning

1. Were you depressed? YES ☐ NO ☐

2. Were you sleepy? YES ☐ NO ☐

3. Were you tired? YES ☐ NO ☐

Day Ruler 24 • Date:

09.00 10.00 11.00 12.00 13.00 14.00 15.00 16.00 17.00 18.00 19.00 20.00 21.00

activity

Notes

Medication

Sleep

→ Going to bed (with the intention to sleep)

[Start trying to go to sleep

↓ Going to sleep

| Tranquil and quiet sleep

← Getting up

⌐ Stop trying to sleep

↑ Waking up

∿∿∿ Broken, wakeful sleep

Activity

A Alcohol
C Caffeine
F Food
M Medicine
S Smoking
E Exercise
D Dreams
N Nightmares
I Interruption
L Lavatory
P Pain/Discomfort
W Worries
T Television/Radio
R Reading

25 NIGHT / DAY

Night Ruler 25 • Date:

21.00 22.00 23.00 24.00 01.00 02.00 03.00 04.00 05.00 06.00 07.00 08.00 09.00

activity

Complete promptly in the morning

not refreshed
almost unwell   OK   very refreshed

0   1   2   3   4   5   6   7   8   9   10

When you woke this morning

1. Were you depressed?   YES ☐   NO ☐
2. Were you sleepy?   YES ☐   NO ☐
3. Were you tired?   YES ☐   NO ☐

Day Ruler 25 • Date:

09.00 10.00 11.00 12.00 13.00 14.00 15.00 16.00 17.00 18.00 19.00 20.00 21.00

activity

Notes

Medication

Sleep

→   Going to bed (with the intention to sleep)
[Start trying to go to sleep
↓   Going to sleep
| Tranquil and quiet sleep
←   Getting up
]   Stop trying to sleep
↑   Waking up
〰   Broken, wakeful sleep

Activity

A   Alcohol
C   Caffeine
F   Food
M   Medicine
S   Smoking
E   Exercise
D   Dreams
N   Nightmares
I   Interruption
L   Lavatory
P   Pain/Discomfort
W   Worries
T   Television/Radio
R   Reading

Sleep

↓	Going to bed (with the intention to sleep)
[	Start trying to go to sleep
↓	Going to sleep
|	Tranquil and quiet sleep
↑	Getting up
⌐	Stop trying to sleep
↑	Waking up
〰	Broken, wakeful sleep

Activity

A	Alcohol
C	Caffeine
F	Food
M	Medicine
S	Smoking
E	Exercise
D	Dreams
N	Nightmares
I	Interruption
L	Lavatory
P	Pain/Discomfort
W	Worries
T	Television/Radio
R	Reading

Night Ruler 26 • Date:

21.00 22.00 23.00 24.00 01.00 02.00 03.00 04.00 05.00 06.00 07.00 08.00 09.00

activity

Complete promptly in the morning

not refreshed
almost unwell   OK   very refreshed

0 1 2 3 4 5 6 7 8 9 10

When you woke this morning

1. *Were you depressed?* YES ☐ NO ☐
2. *Were you sleepy?* YES ☐ NO ☐
3. *Were you tired?* YES ☐ NO ☐

Day Ruler 26 • Date:

09.00 10.00 11.00 12.00 13.00 14.00 15.00 16.00 17.00 18.00 19.00 20.00 21.00

activity

Notes

Medication

Night Ruler 27 • Date:

21.00 22.00 23.00 24.00 01.00 02.00 03.00 04.00 05.00 06.00 07.00 08.00 09.00

activity

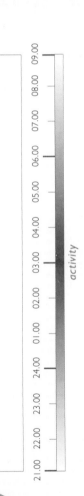

Complete promptly in the morning

not refreshed
almost unwell

OK

very refreshed

0 1 2 3 4 5 6 7 8 9 10

When you woke this morning

1. *Were you depressed?* YES ☐ NO ☐
2. *Were you sleepy?* YES ☐ NO ☐
3. *Were you tired?* YES ☐ NO ☐

Day Ruler 27 • Date:

09.00 10.00 11.00 12.00 13.00 14.00 15.00 16.00 17.00 18.00 19.00 20.00 21.00

activity

Notes

Medication

Sleep

→	Going to bed (with the intention to sleep)
[	Start trying to go to sleep
↓	Going to sleep
|	Tranquil and quiet sleep
←	Getting up
⅂	Stop trying to sleep
↑	Waking up
〰	Broken, wakeful sleep

Activity

A	Alcohol
C	Caffeine
F	Food
M	Medicine
S	Smoking
E	Exercise
D	Dreams
N	Nightmares
I	Interruption
L	Lavatory
P	Pain/Discomfort
W	Worries
T	Television/Radio
R	Reading

28
NIGHT
DAY

Night Ruler 28 • Date:

21.00	22.00	23.00	24.00	01.00	02.00	03.00	04.00	05.00	06.00	07.00	08.00	09.00

activity

Complete promptly in the morning

not refreshed
almost unwell   OK   very
refreshed

0   1   2   3   4   5   6   7   8   9   10

When you woke this morning

1. *Were you depressed?*   YES ☐   NO ☐
2. *Were you sleepy?*   YES ☐   NO ☐
3. *Were you tired?*   YES ☐   NO ☐

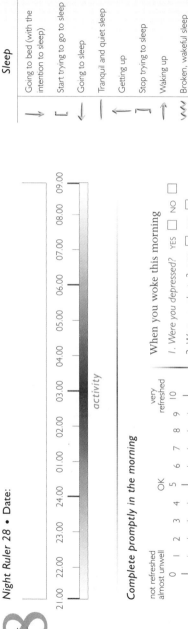

Day Ruler 28 • Date:

09.00	10.00	11.00	12.00	13.00	14.00	15.00	16.00	17.00	18.00	19.00	20.00	21.00

activity

Notes

Medication

Sleep

→	Going to bed (with the intention to sleep)
[	Start trying to go to sleep
↓	Going to sleep
|	Tranquil and quiet sleep
←	Getting up
]	Stop trying to sleep
↑	Waking up
∿	Broken, wakeful sleep

Activity

A	Alcohol
C	Caffeine
F	Food
M	Medicine
S	Smoking
E	Exercise
D	Dreams
N	Nightmares
I	Interruption
L	Lavatory
P	Pain/Discomfort
W	Worries
T	Television/Radio
R	Reading

The questions The questions below do not by themselves provide a definitive assessment of character, mood, or the cause of the sleep disorder, but they do offer clues. These are not quantitive tools, but qualitative. Definitive assessments should be obtained through professional services, but this book may provide the answers that will allow you to help yourself.

The questions give you a framework against which to assess the results from your day and night rulers, ratings scales and daily questions. It is worthwhile completing these questions early on in your assessment in case you find that you are scoring high on a measure such as anxiety or alcoholism. If this is the case then you might want to seek help for this. Completing the sleep diaries and then following the instructions on how to improve your sleep should strengthen your sleep, even though they do not tackle your core difficulty.

These questions ask for "yes" or "no" responses (tick the relevant column). "Don't know" is not an option. The appraisals are found on page 106.

Depressed mood		
Questions	*YES*	*NO*
I am bothered by things that used not to bother me		
I think my life has been a failure		
I am not happy most of the time		
I don't socialize as much as I used to		
I feel lonely		
I don't enjoy life		
I feel sad		
I am depressed most of the time		
I can't concentrate on anything		

Anxiety

Questions	YES	NO
I am usually apprehensive		
I can't relax easily		
I suffer from tense muscles		
My mouth is often dry		
I suffer from diarrhea quite often		
I often sweat a lot during the day		
I often feel on edge		
I often get butterflies in my stomach		
I am often anxious		

Alcoholism

Have you ever had a problem with alcohol ?		
Have you ever been told by friends that you have a problem with alcohol?		
Have you ever been told by friends or relatives that you drink too much alcohol?		
Do you consume more than 3 alcoholic drinks in the evening?		
Do you drink alcohol before bedtime to put yourself to sleep?		

Worry-centered insomnia

I worry before I go to bed that I will sleep badly		
If I wake up in the middle of the night I worry about getting back to sleep		
My mind keeps turning things over		
My thinking takes a long time to "unwind"		

Worry-centered insomnia cont.		
Questions	*YES*	*NO*
Often when I am half asleep I am still trying to follow the train of my thoughts		
I cannot empty my mind before going to sleep		

Tense insomnia		
I find it hard to let go		
My body is full of tension		
I find it difficult to physically relax my body		
I suffer from tension headaches		
My muscles ache all the time		
My back is often painful		

Stimulus-control insomnia		
When I get into bed I often feel more awake		
I spend time reading/watching TV in bed when I should be sleeping		
I sleep better when I am not in my own bed		
I often fall asleep in the living-room		

Sleep-centered insomnia		
I can't concentrate unless I have slept well		
A bad night's sleep leaves me exhausted the next day		
I feel dissatisfied with the depth of my sleep		
I can't cope unless I have slept well		
I know I will feel unwell if I don't sleep properly		
I look awful if I haven't slept properly		

Biological clock: phase advance

Questions	YES	NO
I tire quickly in the evening		
I keep going to bed earlier and earlier		
I can't get my sleep into a proper routine		
I can't control my sleep		
I don't understand why my bedtime seems to be getting earlier and earlier		

Biological clock: phase delay

I don't feel tired enough at bedtime		
My bedtime gets later during the week		
I can't wake up when I want to		
My brain doesn't function until lunch-time		
I keep going to bed later and later		

Drugs and medicines: hypnotics

Have you taken medicines for your nerves recently?		
Do you have to take more pills to feel any effect?		
Have you ever been prescribed medicines for sleep?		
Do you have problems stopping taking sleeping pills?		

Drugs and medicines: social abuse

Do you take drugs regularly?		
Have you ever taken illegal drugs?		
If you consume illegal drugs is it recreational or does your life revolve around them?		
Have you consumed illegal drugs recently?		

Appraisals   If you have answered yes to three or more questions in any section, reconsider how you have filled in the questionnaire and how long you have been feeling this way, and follow the advice given below.

Depressed mood   If you have previously been treated for depression, then you may score higher on this table. If your current mood is poor then consider seeking further help. Depression is often associated with early morning awakening and some phase-advance (*see page* 141) of the sleep-awake cycle.

Anxiety   If you have previously been treated for anxiety then you should consider and act on the advice and treatment that has been effective before. Try the relaxation exercises included in this book and on the tape (*see pages* 119–127).

Alcoholism   If you have been treated for alcoholism then continue with the other sections and consider how to strengthen your sleep. Sleep studies indicate that it may take a year or longer for sleep to recover from chronic alcoholism.

Worry-centered insomnia   Are you a worrier? Worry can increase the state of alertness. You might consider tackling worry directly as well as using the exercises that may displace your worries (*see pages* 124–126). You should also double-check the biological clock questions. It is possible that you are being woken up by this (and possibly other causes such as pain, needing to go to the lavatory, and so on), and because you are awake, you are spending your time worrying.

Tense insomnia   If on balance you feel that tension is a significant factor then you should certainly use the progressive muscular relaxation exercise featured on Side B of the tape (*see also page* 124). You might also consider the responses under "worry-centered insomnia," as worry can lead to tension.

Stimulus-control insomnia   If on the whole you agree with the overall direction of the questions asked, you may have conditioned yourself to remaining awake in bed as opposed to sleeping. The chances are that other factors are involved, but if your insomnia started with a significant life-event such as bereavement, and you had slept well before, plus there is no medical history that might explain the sleeplessness, then it is possible that sleeplessness caused by the life-event has turned into an insomnia. There is a specific way of tackling this: Bootzin Stimulus Control (see page 120).

Sleep-centered insomnia

If on balance this describes you, then refer to the section on inappropriate sleep-inducing behaviors and beliefs (see page 127). It is likely that you will have scored highly on one or more of the other insomnia tables as well, so you could try some of the suggestions associated with those tables. Finally, if all else fails, you should go back and review Chapters One, Two, and Three.

Biological clock: phase advance

If on balance this describes you, then you may be suffering from a biological clock that is running too quickly. See the section on circadian disorders and phase advance in particular (see page 141).

Biological clock: phase delay

If on balance this describes you, then your biological clock may be running too slowly. See the section on circadian disorders and phase delay in particular (see page 141).

Drugs and medicines

If on balance this describes you, it suggests that you have developed an insomnia syndrome. You will probably have scored highly in some of the other tables, so apply the solutions you find there. Also read the section on sleeping pills (see page 114). Chronic insomniacs often find themselves on a cycle of misuse of hypnotics and inadvertently perpetuate their problems. Is caffeine the problem (see page 42)?

So many medicines affect sleep that it is surprising there are not more problems. Clearly, the advice for drugs of abuse and social drugs is to control their intake (you need specialist advice for this). In the case of conventional medicines, you should go back to Chapters One and Two and work out how to strengthen your own sleep system to overcome the disturbing effects of your medication.

Chapter Six

Dealing with disturbed sleep

This chapter now helps you to evaluate what you have learned from the diary and questionnaires, and helps you to decide whether you are suffering from true insomnia, or some other sleep disorder. It suggests some exercises that can help promote sleep. Here too, the tape is introduced, and this has further exercises on it, which can form part of your sleep strategy.

The diagram opposite illustrates many of the ideas introduced in the earlier chapters. Its purpose is to help you understand why some therapeutic strategies work, and some do not. The main points are:

• In some people, a reaction to stress is to tense their muscles. Increased muscle tension increases pressure from the awake system that prevents sleep from taking place.

• Other people have medical problems that produce muscle rigidity, and this has the same effect of preventing sleep.

• Some may have worries that partially activate the fright/ flight systems. These also promote activity in the awake system and so prevent sleep.

• Intrusive thoughts and emotional imagery may activate the arousal systems and/or increase muscle tension, resulting in increased activity in the awake system.

Finally, the biological clock may influence either sleep onset time or waking up time. This depends on heredity, as well as early learning and subsequent conditioning. If the clock is the problem and is alerting the awake system, then the effectiveness of sleep-control techniques such as muscle relaxation, abdominal breathing, meditation and so on,

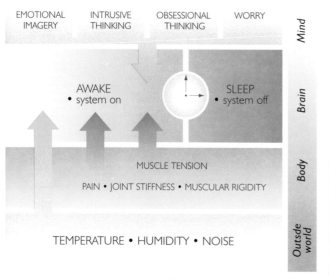

facilitates activity

inhibits activity

There are various factors that can stop you sleeping by increasing activity in the awake system. The exercises and techniques included in this chapter show you how to deal with their input, thus allowing you to go to sleep.

will be limited. It is possible to change your clock, using light. See the section on jet lag (*see page* 53).

You will now have filled in the diary. The first thing to do is to calculate the average amount of time you spend asleep every 24 hours (including naps and times of troubled or light sleep). While you are doing this, see whether there are any consistent patterns to your sleep. The purpose of working out your average amount of sleep is to provide a baseline from which to work on and improve.

Examining the diary rulers

Are there any consistent patterns? Ask yourself the following questions:
• Are weekends having an effect on my sleep?
• How much coffee do I consume (*see page* 42)?
• How much alcohol do I drink (*see page* 44)?
• How many cigarettes do I smoke (*see page* 45)?
• Are soft drugs affecting my sleep (*see page* 45)?
• Is sex a problem? Should I discuss it with my partner?
Start by looking for the obvious, and if that doesn't lead anywhere then consider whether it is a combination of factors that is causing the problem. Remember that one

disturbed night will also affect the next, and sometimes even the following night. This will happen even if the sleep-awake and clock systems are all operating normally.

Are most nights the same? For chronic insomniacs the nights are often different. This inconsistency is regarded by some as the hallmark of insomnia.

Frequent patterns: individual nights

If your night-time rulers generally look like one of the two shown below and you wake up quickly, feel refreshed and don't feel you have a problem—then you don't! Short sleepers tend to have less light sleep (stage 2) than average or long sleepers, and conversely long sleepers tend to have more light sleep. As this stage appears to act simply as a "filler," having more or less is probably not important. Short sleepers can enjoy the extra time awake to pursue other activities. Long sleepers should simply enjoy their long stay in bed. If long sleepers need to remain awake, they must remember that the pressure for sleep will remain, and so they should be vigilant if they are involved in monotonous work. Other variations of normal sleep are illustrated in Chapter Three.

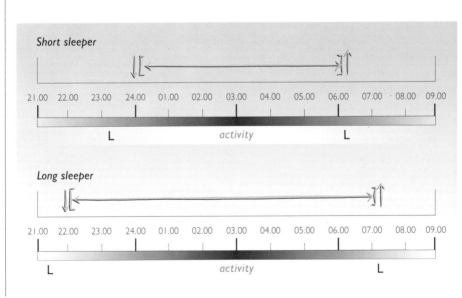

If your sleep seems sound, but you consistently wake up unrefreshed and feel tired and sleepy during the day; if you find that you fall asleep easily on buses, trains, watching TV and so on, then you might be suffering from a disorder that is disturbing your sleep, but not sufficiently to wake you up. The cause might be your bed. Your bed is certainly suspect if you suffer from aches and pains for the first few hours after getting up and subsequently feel better. The wrong sheets, pillows or duvets, uncomfortable bedroom temperature, humidity and so on may all cause these problems.

Unrefreshing sleep

Talking to your bed-partner might help identify what is going on. If you are snoring or occasionally hold your breath, you should go to the section on snoring and sleep apnea (*see page* 135). If you move your legs around a lot during the night then you should read about Periodic Limb Movement Disorder (*see page* 140).

If your ruler looks like the one below, you have a sleep onset problem. Do you have any routines that help to settle you down before going to bed? (*see page* 40). Do you drink coffee or any other drink containing caffeine in the evening? Do you exercise shortly before going to bed? If the problem occurs just on Sundays, read the section on weekend effect (*see page* 112) and try to maintain a more regular schedule. The ruler also shows more than one hour in bed without trying to sleep. This can weaken the association between bed and sleeping, so follow the instructions for "stimulus control" (*see page* 120).

Sleep onset problems

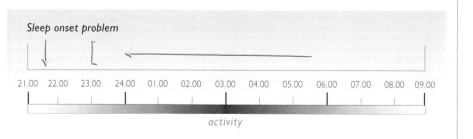

Sleep onset problem

| 21.00 | 22.00 | 23.00 | 24.00 | 01.00 | 02.00 | 03.00 | 04.00 | 05.00 | 06.00 | 07.00 | 08.00 | 09.00 |

activity

Early morning awakening Are you a short sleeper who is going to bed too early? Are you or have you been depressed (*see questionnaire, page 102*)? Follow the stimulus control instructions (*see page 120*) to prevent a negative association developing between bed and sleep. Depression is associated with disrupted sleep, but curiously sleep deprivation can also relieve depression, particularly in those who are most depressed in the morning and whose depression lifts during the day. Depression may speed up the biological clock, which also leads to early morning waking. Exposure to evening light (or bright artificial light) may help slow the clock down and enable you to sleep longer in the morning. Do note, however, that the duration of sleep also decreases with age.

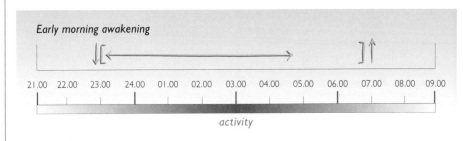

Early morning awakening

activity

Frequent patterns: several nights The page opposite illustrates the weekend effect, when small changes in your routine are sufficient to disrupt your sleep. Friday night shows a slightly later night than usual with just one nightcap (**A**). Waking up on Saturday morning is approximately 2 hours later than this person's usual weekday time. This increase reflects a sleep debt that has probably accumulated during the week.

The various activities on Saturday are omitted, although an exercise session is noted after lunch. Saturday evening involves more alcohol consumption than usual and a much later bedtime. Sleep onset is rapid but sleep is broken in the morning, partly because of the rebound effect of alcohol, also the need to go to the lavatory which is also caused by the alcohol, and because of the biological clock. Nevertheless, broken sleep is achieved until mid-morning.

The Weekend Effect

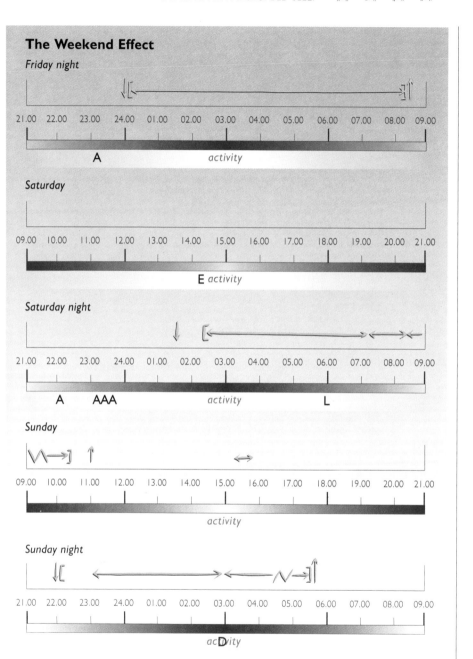

Friday night

21.00 22.00 23.00 24.00 01.00 02.00 03.00 04.00 05.00 06.00 07.00 08.00 09.00

A   activity

Saturday

09.00 10.00 11.00 12.00 13.00 14.00 15.00 16.00 17.00 18.00 19.00 20.00 21.00

E activity

Saturday night

21.00 22.00 23.00 24.00 01.00 02.00 03.00 04.00 05.00 06.00 07.00 08.00 09.00

A   AAA   activity   L

Sunday

09.00 10.00 11.00 12.00 13.00 14.00 15.00 16.00 17.00 18.00 19.00 20.00 21.00

activity

Sunday night

21.00 22.00 23.00 24.00 01.00 02.00 03.00 04.00 05.00 06.00 07.00 08.00 09.00

activity

113

The disrupted nature of the night's sleep, and sleep occurring at a different clock time, leads to a sleep need that is partly dissipated by a mid-afternoon nap (which lessens sleep need the following evening).

Sunday night starts off with a habitual bedtime but the late mornings have probably caused a slight shift in the biological clock which prevents sleep taking place rapidly. Once sleep does begin it is less stable than usual and ends with the Monday morning alarm call. The week starts with a tired and depressed groan. Sound familiar?

This example contained a celebratory amount of alcohol on the Saturday night, but even without the alcohol, some people may find that their change in sleep pattern during the weekend is sufficient to disrupt their sleep at the beginning of the working week. Seasonal daylight savings can produce measurable changes with a shift of only one hour.

The Sunday daytime nap is less of a problem for someone who is always striving to reduce a chronic sleep debt. An afternoon nap is unlikely to affect the biological clock, has the benefit of increasing alertness during the rest of the waking day, and is unlikely to reduce the pressure for sleep during the night.

Occasional use of sleeping pills The sequence of night rulers opposite illustrates what happens to someone who occasionally takes sleeping pills that have been prescribed by a medical practitioner. Most regulatory prescribing bodies recommend only short courses of sleeping pills. The value of this recommendation is not debated here. What is illustrated is someone with chronic insomnia who is trying to manage on a reduced intake of sleeping pills.

On night 1, he falls asleep quickly without a pill, but wakes up and go to the lavatory. On returning to bed he finds his sleep is disturbed, so he takes half a sleeping pill! This is very wrong (but in my experience happens surprisingly often). First, most—although not all—sleeping pills are designed to maintain sleep throughout the night. Taking a pill halfway through the night almost certainly means that there will be a hangover effect the next day.

Occasional use of sleeping pills

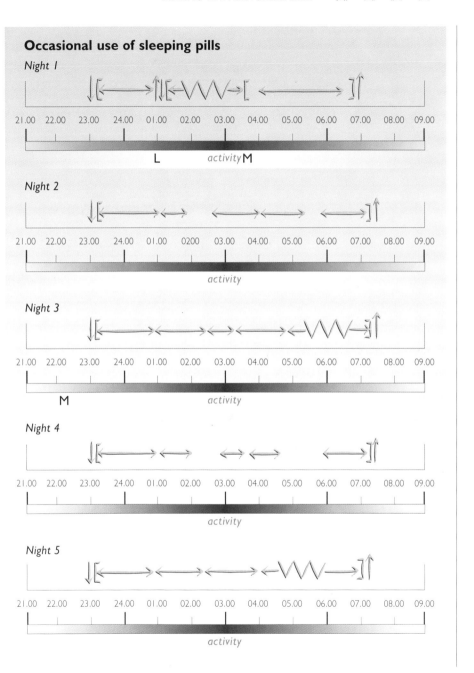

Hangover effects are not only unpleasant but can be dangerous, because of reduced alertness. Secondly, the dosage is calculated carefully to induce sleep quickly and maintain that sleep. Taking half a pill may not induce sleep, and may not maintain it, but it can have sufficient strength to produce a hangover! Many chronic insomniacs become tolerant to their sleeping pills and so they increase the dose. For others who have become tolerant, the ritual of taking the pill is enough to put them back to sleep. In the situation illustrated here, it is likely that the effect of the drug is as much psychological as it is pharmacological.

Night 2 is almost a guilt night. Listening to the doctor's instructions, and feeling guilty about having taken a sleeping pill the night before, the insomniac has a night of broken sleep. One of the reasons is the sleeping pill taken the night before—rebound wakefulness (see page 48). On the third night the insomniac gives in and takes a sleeping pill. It's not a great night's sleep but there is more of it than before. Unfortunately, on the fourth night rebound wakefulness and the reduced sleep-need combine to give the insomniac a rough night's sleep.

The insomniac perseveres without a pill on night 5, and although his sleep is broken, there can be more of it. Some sleeping pills have an impact on sleep two nights afterwards, so insomniacs may have a poor night even on this night. On night 6 the insomniac again takes a pill, and the 2–3 night cycle restarts. This shows that for some people intermittent use of sleeping pills may prolong insomnia.

Your doctor should give you advice on how to use sleeping pills properly. Generally the advice is not to remain on sleeping pills for extended periods. Taking short courses (from a few days to 1–2 weeks) is straightforward, bearing in mind that the majority will cause temporary rebound wakefulness when you stop. Intermittent use is more complex, because of the possibility of rebound effects as shown above, both for physiological reasons (the sleep and awake systems) and pharmalogical (the brain responding to the absence of the sleeping pill). Knowing that these effects exist should allow you to take control.

The rulers below illustrate a rarer sleep problem: narcolepsy. It shows an individual who has disturbed sleep and naps frequently during the day. These naps are extremely difficult to resist and are occasionally irresistible. The pattern of dreaming is also unusual, as dreams are reported at the beginning of sleep. For narcolepsy, see page 134.

Less frequent pattern: narcolepsy

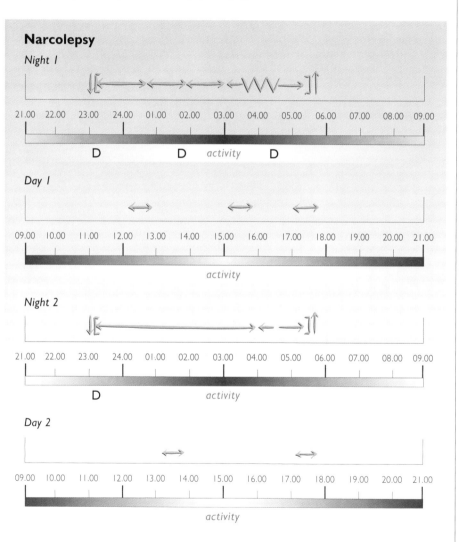

Narcolepsy

Night 1

21.00 22.00 23.00 24.00 01.00 02.00 03.00 04.00 05.00 06.00 07.00 08.00 09.00

D   D   activity   D

Day 1

09.00 10.00 11.00 12.00 13.00 14.00 15.00 16.00 17.00 18.00 19.00 20.00 21.00

activity

Night 2

21.00 22.00 23.00 24.00 01.00 02.00 03.00 04.00 05.00 06.00 07.00 08.00 09.00

D   activity

Day 2

09.00 10.00 11.00 12.00 13.00 14.00 15.00 16.00 17.00 18.00 19.00 20.00 21.00

activity

Now what do I do?

Problem	Ruler indications	Action
Alcoholism	Light sleep	Use the diary to get an understanding of your sleep, and check the section 'Why can't I fall asleep' (see page 50) to ensure that you have not developed other habits or addictions that may be weakening your sleep. Seek further help for your alcohol intake.
Depression	Early morning waking and/or sleep onset and/or disturbed sleep	Depression is often associated with early morning waking and fragmented sleep. As with alcoholism, make sure you are not doing anything to weaken your sleep: see 'Why can't I fall asleep?' (page 50). Also consider the treatment for phase advance (see right). Seek further help for the depression.
Anxiety	Pre-sleep wakefulness	Anxiety is often associated with muscle tension, so use the relaxation exercise found on the tape (Side B). This technique can be extended by using autogenic training (see page 124). See also "worry-centered insomnia" (page 106). Seek help for further anxiety relief measures.
Social drugs, sleeping pills and medicines	Complex	Learn to understand your sleep and how it may be affected by prescribed, pharmacy, social, or abused drugs. See also the section on sleeping pills (page 46).
Worry-centered insomnia	Pre-sleep wakefulness and sleep maintenance	Many chronic insomniacs worry about their sleep. The advice is always not to worry specifically about the lack of sleep, but supplement with worry-reduction exercises (see page 120) or meditation exercises, or thought-blocking techniques such as chanting a mantra (found on Side A of the tape). Breathing and relaxation exercises (see page 120) will also help.
Tense insomnia	Pre-sleep wakefulness	Try to identify source of tension: physical (posture, bed, mattress) or mental (reaction to stresses of day). Progresssive muscle relaxation (tape Side B) or autogenic training (see page 124) will help. If anxiety is part of the problem, seek further help for this.
Stimulus-control insomnia	Pre-sleep wakefulness	If associated with your bed and bedroom use Bootzin Stimulus Control method (see page 120) to break down the connection.

Now what do I do?

Problem	Ruler indications	Action
Sleep-centered insomnia	Pre-sleep wakefulness and maintenance	Sleep-centered and worry-centered insomnia often go hand in hand (see methods for worry-centered above). Paradoxical intention (see page 127) can also help.
Phase delay	Pre-sleep	If mild, then simply adjusting wake up and rise time may be sufficient to increase pressure on sleep. Regularity is important. If more severe, see section on phase delay (page 141).
Phase advance	Morning wakenings	If mild, adjusting bedtime, by staying up, may be enough to increase pressure on sleep. Regularity is important. If more severe, see section on phase advance (page 141).
Snoring	Disturbed sleep	If sleep apnea is suspected, consult your doctor, especially if daytime sleepiness is severe. See strategies for dealing with snoring and apnea (page 136).
Narcolepsy	Disturbed sleep	See "Sleep disorders" (Chapter Seven).

Techniques to help the insomniac

This book provides a framework and context for the use of various techniques, and because it is a kit it provides first-aid which can be applied straight away. You must do the assessments in Chapter Five before you start using the following techniques. Using the wrong ones may do nothing for your sleep and could just make you feel frustrated.

The tape

The tape includes a selection of easy-to-follow relaxation exercises that you can try at home. On Side A you will find simple routines (a deep-breathing exercise, a guided visualization, and a mantra) that help to alleviate anxiety and tension—common factors that contribute to poor sleep. You can use these routines during the day or night—whenever you want to feel really relaxed. Side B includes a progressive muscular relaxation exercise specifically designed to help you go to sleep (see also page 122). I recommend that you read the rest of this chapter before you listen to the tape.

Bootzin Stimulus Control Richard Bootzin, Northwestern University, Chicago, devised this technique more than 20 years ago, to counteract conditioned insomnia.

Problems with falling asleep (young to middle-aged adults)
1. Lie down in your bed to sleep only when feeling sleepy.
2. Use the bed only for sleep (sex is the only exception).
3. If you are unable to sleep in about 10 minutes, get up and ideally leave the bedroom.
4. Return to bed once sleepy and follow instruction 3.
5. Set the alarm to get up at the same time every day.
6. Do not nap during the day.

Problems with falling asleep (adults 60 years and older)
1. Lie down in your bed to sleep only when feeling sleepy.
2. Use the bed only for sleep (sex is the only exception).
3. If you are unable to sleep in about 20 minutes, get up and ideally leave the bedroom.
4. Return to bed once sleepy and follow instruction 3.

Problems with staying asleep
1. Get up once awake for 10–20 minutes, then follow the falling asleep instructions above.

The purpose of the above instructions is to reduce the association between bed and being awake, to establish an association between bed and falling asleep, and to re-establish the sequence of being sleepy and falling asleep.

Relaxing The link between muscle tension and sleeplessness has been noted a number of times. Once sleeplessness becomes a problem, and problems are faced by increasing tension, then a vicious cycle begins.

Deep breathing It is easy to become tense through the day. Deep breathing (diaphragmatic breathing) is a well-established relaxation technique. It can be done at almost any time and anywhere. There is also a deep-breathing exercise on Side A of the tape.
• If you have never practiced deep breathing it is best to start on your back.
• Lie down and put one hand on your chest and the other on your abdomen.

Your legs should either be comfortably outstretched or, if you prefer, bent at the knees with your feet flat on the floor (see below).

Inhale slowly through the nose.

Feel the hand on your chest rise.

When the breath reaches your stomach, push your abdomen upwards letting your other hand rise slightly higher than the hand on your chest. The abdomen is raised by the diaphragm expanding.

Hold for one second, then reverse the process. Exhale and allow your muscle to relax and let the air out of your chest and nostrils. Relax your jaw as you exhale.

As you learn to control your breathing, start concentrating on the breath as you exhale. Appreciate it. Was it smooth, warm, luxurious? How did it feel against your nostrils, your lips? Was it comfortable?

• Sometimes intrusive thoughts will break your concentration on your breathing. Banish them. Don't get angry or frustrated. Think about them as if they are written down on paper. Put the paper in a bottle and throw it into the sea—let them float away.

Do your breathing exercise for 10 minutes twice a day. Try to develop it as a routine. If your body tenses up, do the breathing exercise. Be vigilant to tension. If you become tense, close your eyes and focus on your breathing.

If you have difficulty in identifying movement in your stomach, then try putting a book on it, and force it to go

Once you are lying comfortably on your back you can begin the exercise. Remember: the hand on your abdomen should rise up slightly higher than the hand on your chest before you exhale.

up. Some people find that by doing this, and putting their hands behind their heads, it helps to identify the right muscle to use to execute the movement.

It is best to practice abdominal breathing during the day until you get it right. As you get more proficient, you may get butterflies in your stomach, or feel as if you are floating. It is worth persevering, as these sensations should become pleasant ones. The more pleasant they become the more likely you are to go to sleep. If you feel light-headed or dizzy then you may not be breathing fast enough, and not enough oxygen is getting into your body.

If you are unwell, for whatever reason, it is worth trying the exercise once, for about half an hour and no more. This is to prevent an association developing between the exercise and feelings of frustration and failure.

Variations   Abdominal breathing can be done anywhere, any time, but practicing on your back is usually the easiest way to learn. You could do it in the sitting or standing position, but it is more difficult to feel your abdomen. You can also do the exercise by lying on your stomach with your arms folded in front of your body. Your hands should rest on your biceps. In this position, your chest should not touch the floor. You should feel your abdomen expanding.

On-the-spot deep breathing   You may become aware of your muscles tensing up—shoulders, back, abdomen, or jaw are all common areas. Deep breathing may help stop the tension developing.
• Inhale slowly, pushing the stomach muscles out.
• Exhale slowly, feeling the stomach muscles collapse.
• As you exhale repeat either a calming or neutral phrase to yourself: for example, "relax," or, "quiet," or "still." It doesn't matter what the word or phrase is.

Progressive muscular relaxation   Side B of the tape gives instruction in progressive muscular relaxation. This technique is useful for problems with going to sleep and problems with returning to sleep after waking up. The muscle groups involved are listed in the box at the top of the next page.

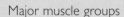

Major muscle groups

The following muscle groups are used in progressive muscular relaxation and autogenic training:

- *Hip and legs:* feet, calves, thighs, buttocks

- *Torso:* lower back, stomach/abdomen, chest

- *Arms:* hands, forearms, biceps

- *Head and shoulders:* shoulders, neck, throat, head

- *Face:* jaws, tongue, lips, nose, cheeks, eyes, brow, scalp

---

If you also use the variations (*given below*), progressive muscular relaxation can take a while to work through—perhaps a month, or even longer. Coupled with other sensible sleep-promoting techniques, it may provide a long-term and enduring solution to the sleep difficulties of a chronic insomniac.

The technique can be elaborated further by working on both legs or both hands simultaneously. This provides a variation that may prevent the technique from becoming too monotonous or boring. Monotony and boredom are soporific for some but irritating for others.

Variations on progressive muscular relaxation

Yet another variation is to work on diagonal groups of muscles at the same time. This is called differential relaxation. It involves working with two of the major groups of muscles (*see box above*). It could start with tensing the right arm and hand while simultaneously relaxing the left foot and calf, followed by tensing the left foot and calf and relaxing the right hand and arm. This is then followed by tensing the left arm and hand while simultaneously relaxing the right foot and calf, and finally relaxing the left arm and hand while tensing the right foot and calf. These routines can also be applied to the other major muscle groups; you can work with any combination.

Autogenic training

Autogenic training uses the same muscle groups as progressive muscular relaxation. It allows you to learn to self-generate feelings of warmth and relaxation. Time must be set aside—at least 20 minutes a day for each main muscle group. Spend a week practicing before trying out this technique in the evening.

Autogenic training routine

Find a quiet spot where you will not be interrupted. The aim is to invoke feelings of warmth and heaviness, and so feel relaxed and ready for sleep. Use a reclining chair, or lie down flat. Wear something loose and comfortable. Take a breath and release it slowly. Another breath, and exhale. Another breath, and exhale. Your right arm and hand should be lying straight beside you or on the arm of the chair. Concentrate on your muscles and joints, feel their warmth and weight while repeating the phrases (*opposite*).

Pre-sleep mental exercises and thought blocking

Whether you have a quiet day or a busy day, various thoughts ebb and flow through your mind. These thoughts have to be dealt with, otherwise they may emerge at bedtime. Also, you may fall asleep quickly but wake up later on, and the various thoughts of things to do, matters to

Relaxation techniques such as progressive muscular relaxation and autogenic training help to overcome factors that can keep the awake system active, and by doing so allow sleep to take place.

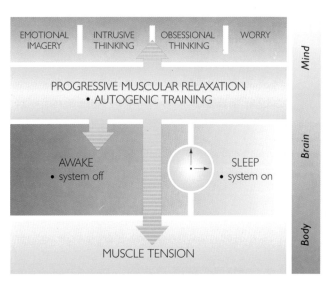

Key

facilitates activity

inhibits activity

Autogenic training routine

Once you have followed the preparatory instructions on page 124 you are ready to begin.

- My right hand is feeling heavy.
- My right hand is heavy and warm.
- My right hand is resting.
- My right arm is feeling heavy.
- My right arm is heavy and warm.
- My right arm is resting.

Repeat the above phrases twice. Feel your arm float out on its own, from the shoulders, to the elbow to the tips of your fingers.

Now switch to the other side.

- My left hand is feeling heavy.
- My left hand is heavy and warm.
- My left hand is resting.
- My left arm is feeling heavy.
- My left arm is heavy and warm.
- My left arm is resting.

Once you have finished this, and you feel even more relaxed, then stay still for a little while longer. Appreciate the feeling.

After several days of working with arms and hands, you can move on to your legs. Use the same kind of phrases and techniques. You are aiming to elicit feelings of heaviness, lightness or floating.

- My right foot is feeling heavy.
- My right foot is heavy and warm.
- My right foot is resting.
- My right leg is feeling heavy.
- My right leg is heavy and warm.
- My right leg is resting.
- My right thigh is feeling heavy.
- My right thigh is heavy and warm.
- My right thigh is resting.
- My right buttock is feeling heavy.

- My right buttock is heavy and warm.
- My right buttock is resting.

Now switch to the other side.

- My left foot is feeling heavy.
- My left foot is heavy and warm.
- My left foot is resting.
- My left leg is feeling heavy.
- My left leg is heavy and warm.
- My left leg is resting.
- My left thigh is feeling heavy.
- My left thigh is heavy and warm.
- My left thigh is resting.
- My left buttock is feeling heavy.
- My left buttock is heavy and warm.
- My left buttock is resting.

After a few days, you add the next muscle group. Again the instructions follow the pattern:

- My stomach is feeling heavy.
- My stomach is heavy and warm.
- My stomach is resting.
- My chest is feeling heavy.
- My chest is heavy and warm.
- My chest is resting.
- My lower back is feeling heavy.
- My lower back is heavy and warm.
- My lower back is resting.

Finally, the last group of muscles is added.

- My shoulders are feeling heavy.
- My shoulders are heavy and warm.
- My shoulders are resting.
- My neck and throat are feeling heavy.
- My neck and throat are heavy and warm.
- My neck and throat are resting.
- My head and face are feeling heavy.
- My head and face are heavy and warm.
- My head and face are resting.

discuss, appointments to arrange, may all flood back. You need to set aside time to deal with these thoughts, so that if they intrude as you try to go to sleep, or if you wake up during the night, you know they have been dealt with.

Before you go to bed, relax, and consider what thoughts need to be handled. Think about thoughts that aren't there. Anticipate worrying thoughts. Note them down so that you won't have forgotten them in the morning. If you recall things that you need to do, write them down, and remind yourself that you will be able to deal with them after you have slept. And after you have written these notes, stop and think again—are there any others you have forgotten? Write them down. Some people like to visualize their thoughts, and then pack them into a box. Close the lid. This exercise should only take 5–10 minutes. Enjoy your uncluttered mind. Use the exercise as part of your bedtime ritual. Teach your body and mind that this is the time for sleep.

Switching your mind off

People with busy lives often like to use their time in bed to think. That's fine if you can go to sleep when you want, but if you're an insomniac you must use your bed just for sleep. Once you have cleared your mind, try to keep it switched off. A thought for an insomniac is like a drink for an alcoholic—once started you can't stop. So don't start. Don't over-focus, though, either. If you find you're thinking about not thinking, try to let the thoughts go. Coast; go into neutral.

Final suggestions

You may want to try some additional techniques such as meditation or mentally chanting mantras (*on the tape*), but to start off with just try the pre-bed exercises described above. Don't think deliberately; let your thoughts subside.

Thought blocking

Sometimes your mind will be very active, or you will wake up in the middle of the night with thoughts flooding in. You need to block these thoughts with something neutral that will keep your attention but will not wake you up. One option is simply to repeat a word slowly, such as "the": the, the, the, the. It can be any word, just something to focus

on, but not enough to wake you up. Some people like to visualize a circle with a light attached on the periphery. The light just goes around and around. It's something to occupy the mind.

This is a technique to help you go to sleep. It is—as the name suggests—a perverse technique. You concentrate on remaining awake and are determined that you will not go to sleep. It helps some people, presumably by blocking out intrusive and alerting thoughts.

Paradoxical intention

If you have worked out that your coffee intake is too high (if you are drinking more than 10 cups per day) then you must reduce your intake. A reduction of half a cup of coffee per day is managed by most who are addicted, without causing side-effects. Use replacements such as hot chocolate or herbal teas. Decaffeinated coffee is not such a good idea, as it is also addictive.

Too much caffeine?

The questions on sleep-centered insomnia focused on various beliefs about sleep (not coping, poor concentration, feeling unwell) that are often associated with the belief that disturbed sleep causes physical and mental harm. There is little evidence for this. Total sleep deprivation causes transient impairment, but most insomniacs actually get their basic biological quota.

Inappropriate behaviors and beliefs

Throw out the bedroom clock. It was explained earlier that sleep is normally broken, but most people are not aware of these brief periods of wakefulness. It is quite possible to sleep and wake up without realizing you have been asleep, and to worry about being awake. If you need an alarm clock, turn it round so that you don't look at it.

If you are particularly dissatisfied with the depth of your sleep then read on in Chapter Seven. Many sleep disorders cause insomnia as well as daytime sleepiness. It is possible that the problem is not insomnia but another condition, such as sleep apnea.

Finally, believe me—you don't look awful. If you still think you do, the cosmetics industry is there to help.

Chapter Seven

Sleep disorders

This book has so far dealt with normal sleep that has been disturbed, either because the individual is mismanaging his or her sleep, or because the role of worker or carer has reduced the ability to cope with disturbed sleep. A good deal of insomnia is controllable, but there comes a point when some people may need to seek extra help. Quite often, they are suffering from a sleep disorder.

Disordered sleep and sleep disorders

On the basis of three main systems—sleep, awake, and clock —this book has described what sleep is, how it works and what goes wrong to create the condition of sleepless ness. The term insomnia has been reserved for chronic sleeplessness without an obvious external or medical cause. This chapter further extends the definition of insomnia and also expands into other sleep disorders. The transition is from disordered sleep to sleep disorders. Sleep disorders have to be considered as often the sufferer is only aware of the insomnia, and the doctor may not be able to detect the source of the problem by interview.

The table on pages 130–131 lists the main categories of disordered sleep and sleep disorders. The tables are almost entirely consistent with the International Classification of Sleep Disorders (1990). Some sleep problems arise when something has gone wrong with the central sleep, awake and clock systems (sleep disorders), while others are caused when something outside these systems has gone wrong, such as in the case of Parkinson's disease, arthritis, depression, dementia, and so on (disordered sleep). Sometimes the categories are not so clearly defined. It is beyond the capacity of this book to deal with all of the

128

isorders listed in the table, and so this chapter will cover st the main disorders (*these are the ones highlighted in bold in the ble overleaf*).

here are at least two types of sleep disorders center: those at concentrate on sleep-related breathing disorders, such ; obstructive sleep apnea (*see page* 135), and those that pro-ide clinical diagnostic services and treatment for all sleep isorders. The latter are usually multidisciplinary and are ore likely to have someone with an interest in insomnia.

he American Sleep Disorders Association (ASDA) provides n accreditation service for sleep disorders centers and lab-ratories. The Association ensures that facilities maintain he highest quality of patient care, and re-accreditation is equired every 5 years. For details of the Association, see Resources" on page 157.

Sleep disorders centers

efore you go to the center you will almost certainly eceive a diary and questionnaire. This book may have been seful, but the center will probably want to use its own ests. After a clinical diagnostic interview the decision to leep in the laboratory may be made.

Overnight monitoring involves gluing multiple elec-rodes (smaller than a dime) on to the scalp to measure rain waves (EEG), eye movement and chin muscle tone. here is no need to be shaved—in fact bald heads are more lifficult as the electrodes tend to skid around when you are rying to apply them! These electrodes provide enough nformation to identify the main stages of sleep. It is also ecessary to measure breathing, as breathing and the level of oxygen in the blood can also disturb sleep. This may nvolve sensors on the nose (air-flow) and fingers (blood-xygen levels), and chest-straps (breathing movements). As limb movements can also disturb sleep, further elec-rodes may also be attached to the legs. This is more or less he standard wiring.

Some centers like to video you as well during the night. This can be helpful in interpreting some of the electro-physiological data. (*Text continues on page 132.*)

What happens when you go to a sleep disorders center?

Sleep Disorders

Type of disorder		Disorder
Sleep Disorders Associated with Medical/Psychiatric Disorders	*Associated with mental disorders*	• Psychoses • Mood disorders • Anxiety disorders • Panic disorders • Alcoholism
	Associated with neurological disorders	• Cerebral degenerative disorders • Dementia • Parkinson's disease • Fatal familial insomnia • Sleep-related epilepsy • Electrical status epilepticus of sleep • Sleep-related headaches
	Associated with other medical disorders	• Sleeping sickness • Nocturnal cardiac ischaemia • Chronic obstructive pulmonary disease • Sleep-related asthma • Sleep-related gastro-oesophageal reflux • Peptic ulcer disease • Fibrositis syndrome
Dyssomnias (produce insomnia or excessive sleepiness)	*Intrinsic sleep disorders*	• **Psychophysiological insomnia** • **Sleep-state misperception** • **Idiopathic insomnia** • **Narcolepsy** • Hypersomnias • **Sleep apnea syndromes** • **Periodic-limb-movement disorder** • **Restless-legs syndrome**
	Extrinsic sleep disorders	• Inadequate sleep hygiene • Environmental sleep disorder • Altitude insomnia • Adjustment sleep disorder • Insufficient sleep syndrome

Sleep Disorders

Type of disorder		Disorder
Dyssomnias (cont.)	Extrinsic sleep disorders (cont.)	• Limit-setting sleep disorder • Sleep-onset association disorder • Food allergy insomnia • Nocturnal eating (drinking) syndrome • Hypnotic-dependent sleep disorder • Stimulant-dependent sleep disorder • Alcohol-dependent sleep disorder • Toxin-induced sleep disorder
	Circadian rhythm sleep disorders	• Time zone (jet lag) syndrome • Shift-work sleep disorder • Irregular sleep-wake pattern • Delayed-sleep-phase syndrome • Advanced-sleep-phase syndrome • Non 24-hour sleep-wake disorder
Parasomnias	Arousal disorders	• Sleepwalking • Night (sleep) terrors • Confusional arousals
	Parasomnias usually associated with REM sleep	• Nightmares • Sleep paralysis • Impaired sleep-related penile erections • Sleep-related painful erections • REM sleep-related sinus arrest • REM sleep behavior disorder
	Other parasomnias	• Sleep bruxism • Sleep enuresis • Sleep-related abnormal swallowing syndrome • Nocturnal paroxysmal dystonia • Sudden unexplained nocturnal death syndrome • Primary snoring • Infant sleep apnea • Sudden infant death syndrome • Benign neonatal sleep myoclonus

This whole procedure is known as nocturnal poly-somnography, and is the major diagnostic tool in sleep disorders. It is used in the evaluation of suspected sleep-related breathing disorders and periodic limb-movement disorder (*see page* 140) and when the cause of insomnia is uncertain, or when behavioral or pharmacological therapies are unsuccessful.

Patients often worry about not being able to sleep in the laboratory. The majority do, particularly if their problem is excessive sleepiness. Conditioned insomniacs may also, embarrassingly, sleep well. This should not be a problem as most centers will be aware of both the pitfalls and the benefits of the measurement techniques used.

Many sleep apneics (*see page* 135) and narcoleptics (*see page* 134) are very sleepy. The Multiple Sleep Latency Test is used to measure this during the day, and simply involves repeated measuring of how long it takes to get to sleep.

Insomnia

The classification identifies three particular insomnias: *psychophysiological insomnia, sleep-state misperception, and idiopathic insomnia.*

Psychophysiological insomnia

Psychophysiological insomnia is also known as learned insomnia or conditioned insomnia, and can be verified using polysomnography. As with many chronic insomnias it is thought to arise in susceptible individuals after some precipitating event. The event may be minor—perhaps not being able to adjust quickly after jet lag, or after a bereavement, or even after a change of job. There is usually one point in time that the patient can identify when their sleep deteriorated. There are usually other factors associated with chronic insomnia which tend to perpetuate the situation. These may arise as a result of trying to cope with the insomnia, or they may always have been present. Many of the factors harmful to good sleep were identified in Chapters Three and Four. Napping is not necessarily the wrong thing to do in this situation, though chronic insomniacs often cannot take naps: whatever keeps them awake during the night also keeps them awake during the day.

Conditioned insomniacs often react to stress by increasing muscle tension, which makes it difficult to fall asleep. On top of this, they also become very focused on their sleep. This creates a very nasty cycle of events: they try to sleep, fail, become tense, fail again, become more tense, and have considerable difficulties ever getting to sleep (*see diagram below*). A learned association between failing to sleep and the bedroom exacerbates their difficulties. Chapter Six covered some of the techniques that can be used to deal with conditioned insomnia, such as the Bootzin Stimulus Control (*page 120*) and the breathing and relaxation exercises. The techniques will work, but if insomnia has become ingrained, and possibly complicated with sleeping-pill dependence, then the help of an expert therapist should be considered.

The existence of sleep-state misperception is disputed. This diagnosis occurs when a patient claims not to have slept at all, yet polysomnography carried out at a sleep center indicates that he or she did. This is a rare situation. Peter Hauri (Mayo Clinic) reports one patient who dreamed that he was awake trying to sleep!

Sleep-state misperception

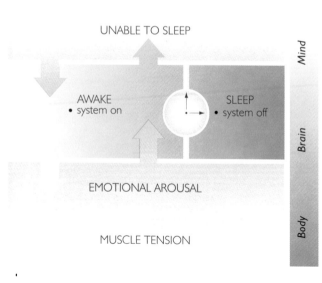

Conditioned insomniacs experience a perpetual cycle of trying to sleep, failing, becoming tense and agitated, then trying to sleep again, and so on, making it difficult for them to ever get to sleep.

Key

facilitates activity

inhibits activity

Idiopathic insomnia This insomnia is also known as childhood onset insomnia. It is a lifelong inability to get adequate sleep and presumably reflects an underactive sleep system or an overactive awake system. This insomnia is unremitting, but the mental state of the sufferer generally remains good. There are no events that trigger this: as far as the patient recalls, he or she has tended to be alert most of the time. Polysomnography shows very poorly formed EEG sleep that is clearly unusual. Treatment involves two simultaneous strategies: firstly, all the methods described in previous chapters have to be employed to increase the possibility of sleep; and secondly, low-dose sedating antidepressants are given (sleeping pills only work occasionally). The low-dose antidepressant is well below the dose required to act as an antidepressant, but these compounds have multiple pharmacological actions, some of which appear to be both beneficial and long-lasting.

Excessive sleep and daytime sleepiness Some people have problems with the ability to control their sleep. Unfortunately in many societies, past and present, they have been labelled as lazy. The National Commission on Sleep Disorders Research reported in 1993 that inappropriate sleepiness during the day cost the US over $15 billion in direct expenses and nearly $70 billion dollars in lost productivity. Telling someone that he or she is lazy is not enough.

Narcolepsy Narcolepsy is inherited—close relatives are 60 times more likely to have narcolepsy, and genetic markers have been identified. It usually develops in late adolescence or early adulthood. The symptoms often emerge slowly.

It is clearly an overactive-sleep-system abnormality over which the narcoleptics have no control. The main symptoms are daytime sleepiness and sudden bouts of muscle weakness, possibly paralysis (often experienced just before falling asleep). Frightening hallucinations can occur at sleep onset, although sometimes it is more of a confusion between knowing whether you are awake and doing something, or dreaming about doing something. Some sufferers can go into automatic mode for many minutes, and then not recall that they are awake. An irony for narcoleptics is that they also often suffer from sleeplessness during the night.

When given the Multiple Sleep Latency Test (MSLT) narcoleptics fall asleep very quickly. An unusual feature of their sleep is that it often begins with REM sleep. This occurs at night as well as on some of the MSLT tests. REM occurring at sleep onset and the muscle paralysis point to something going wrong with the REM control system of the sleep system (*see page 29*).

Narcolepsy does not appear to be common, but estimates of numbers in the US range from 100,000–600,000. It is often left undiagnosed. Narcoleptics are often labeled as lazy, and many have problems holding on to their jobs. Those suffering from mild narcolepsy do not like to admit that sometimes they are not sure whether they are awake or dreaming. For adolescents and youngsters this can be particularly frightening.

Narcolepsy can be treated to a great extent using stimulants such as amphetamines and antidepressants (again, antidepressants are not being used to control depression) to control the muscle paralysis. Taking scheduled naps during the day also reduces the need to sleep and so lessens the number of episodes of uncontrolled sleep. Loss of muscle control can be associated with strong emotions, such as deep joy or anger. This onset of muscle weakness prepares the narcoleptic for a sleep episode, so he or she can try to keep it under control.

Snoring and sleep apnea

Sleep apnea is when someone stops breathing during sleep. The partner will almost certainly be aware of the snoring (sometimes the noise-level of snoring can approach industrial levels of noise pollution!) and will probably have noticed periods when the sleeper has stopped breathing. It is not clear yet whether snoring or sleep apnea and the resulting lowering of blood-oxygen levels are associated with grave medical consequences (studies to investigate this are still being conducted). However, sleep apnea (and possibly snoring) are certainly associated with a greatly increased incidence of highway accidents. The danger from sleep apnea is undeniable—unexpected and involuntary sleep. Highway driving is not kind to the sleepy. Shift-workers, including nurses and doctors, and sleep apneics are all involved in accidents, sometimes fatal, more often than those whose sleep is not impaired.

In obstructive sleep apnea a blockage stops breathing. As the respiratory system detects lowered oxygen levels it increases the muscular effort involved in breathing. As levels drop, increased attempts are made to breathe, and the awake system is drawn in to aid the situation. Sleep begins to lighten. In a major episode, wakefulness may result, but it may be of such a short duration that the person is unaware that he or she has been awake. In more minor episodes, the EEG may not show wakefulness, but it does usually show some activity. These minor disruptions are sufficient to impair sleep so that the person is sleepy the next day.

Snoring in adults Snoring is often viewed as amusing, but it can lead to marital or partnership discord. Here are some tips on how to reduce snoring (and possibly sleep apnea):
• Don't drink alcohol within 5 hours of going to bed.
• Avoid taking sleeping pills and tranquilizers.
• Stop smoking.
• If necessary, lose weight.
• Try sleeping on your side rather than your back.
• Improve nasal breathing.
• Raise the head of the bed.
• An improvement in breathing can be produced by trying a different position during sleep as well as by using a nasal decongestant.
• Use nasal decongestants which do not contain ephedrine or pseudoephedrine (both of these will keep you awake).
• If you are suffering from hayfever, take non-sedating antihistamines to clear the airways.
• Nasal dilators or other devices (*see page* 138) are sometimes useful as well.

Snoring in children should be taken seriously, particularly if the children are sleepy during the day (or are hyperactive), aggressive, and have learning difficulties. Research has found that children with recurring tonsilitis and this pattern of behavior benefit from the surgical removal of their tonsils. Both daytime and night-time behavior resolve and growth spurt may also occur.

Breathing movements might not stop with mild obstructive sleep apnea. In more severe cases patients' breathing may stop, to the extent that their partners are alarmed and wake them up to restart their breathing. Breathing often restarts with loud snores, mumbling noises, and grunting. Body movements also usually occur and sufferers are often described as restless sleepers. Going to the lavatory to urinate also occurs more often as symptoms progress.

When sleep apneic patients wake up they generally feel unrefreshed, and are possibly disoriented, uncoordinated and groggy. Morning headaches, which clear up 1 to 2 hours after waking up, are a common feature. Stories of laziness, lost jobs, and broken marriages abound. Naps are generally not refreshing, in contrast to narcoleptics who find naps very refreshing.

Dr. Murray Johns of Melbourne, Australia designed and validated the Epworth Sleepiness Scale (ESS). It asks a patient to rate the chance of dozing during various daytime activities. Fill in this chart(see page 138), and then go on to answer the questions in the chart on page 139.

After completing the table, review how many questions have been answered yes. If the majority are yes then you may well be suffering from sleep apnea. If a few are yes, but particularly if you are a middle-aged male, with a collar size greater than 17 in (42 cm), who is overweight, snores, and is sleepy during the day (Epworth score 16 or greater), then you are likely to be suffering from sleep apnea.

Therapies can be conservative: weight reduction, stopping smoking, avoiding alcohol and sleeping pills, in fact many of the suggestions listed in the snoring section of this

How sleep apnea causes sleepiness

- Breathing stops, causing increased arousal and a move towards wakefulness.

↓

- The increased arousal causes breathing to restart without conscious awareness returning. However, sleep has been impaired, resulting in increased sleepiness.

Epworth Sleepiness Scale

Therapy for apnea

chapter (*see page 136*). Sometimes apneas are dependent on sleeping position, and adjusting the sleep position may benefit some sufferers. There are no widely accepted pharmacological preparations.

Nasal-CPAP (continuous positive airway pressure) is the main treatment. This involves devices that blow air into the airways at a pressure sufficient to keep the airways open. These devices have been called pneumatic splints. The impact for the patient is almost immediate and usually overnight—they will know when they've been treated successfully. Nasal-CPAP is well tolerated, although some patients or their partners may not find it acceptable. Various surgical and dental treatments do exist, but there is still some doubt as to whether these treatments are really effective or not.

Epworth Sleepiness Scale

In contrast to just feeling tired, how likely are you to doze off or fall asleep in the following situations? (Even if you have not done some of these things recently, try to work out how they would affect you.) Use the following scale to choose the most appropriate number for each situation:

0 = would never doze • 1 = slight chance of dozing • 2 = moderate chance of dozing • 3 = high chance of dozing

Situation	Chance of Dozing
1. Sitting reading	
2. Watching TV	
3. Sitting inactive in a public place (such as the theater)	
4. As a car passenger for an hour without a break	
5. Lying down to rest in the afternoon	
6. Sitting talking to someone	
7. Sitting quietly after lunch without alcohol	
8. In a car, while stopping for a few minutes in traffic	
Total Score	

0–8: normal sleep function • 8–10: mild sleepiness • 11–15: moderate sleepiness • 16–20: severe sleepiness • 21–24: excessive sleepiness

Sleep apnea assessment

Questions		YES	NO
Physical condition	Are you overweight?		
	Do you have high blood pressure?		
	Do you have trouble breathing through your nose?		
	Do you often have a drink of alcohol before going to bed?		
	If you are a man, is your collar size 17 in (42 cm) or larger?		
During the night	Do you snore loudly each night?		
	Have you been told that you stop breathing for 10 seconds or more when you are asleep?		
	Are you a restless sleeper?		
	Do you have to get up several times to urinate?		
Waking up	Do you wake up in the morning tired and "foggy," not ready to face the day?		
	Do you have headaches in the morning?		
	Are you very sleepy during the day?		
During the day	Do you have difficulty concentrating, and completing tasks?		
	Do you carry out routine tasks in a daze?		
	Have you ever arrived home in your car but could not remember the trip from work?		
Emotional life	Are you having serious relationship problems at home, with friends and relatives, or at work?		
	Are you afraid that you may be out of touch with the real world, unable to think clearly, losing your memory, or emotionally ill?		
	Are you irritable and angry, especially first thing in the morning?		

Restless-legs syndrome

Someone suffering from restless-legs syndrome feels as if th[e] need to move their legs. There is often an uncomfortab[le] creeping and crawling or pins and needles sensation de[ep] within the legs or running up and down the legs. This sens[a]tion occurs while awake, usually in the evening at bedtime, [or] during sleep. The movement required to alleviate this feeli[ng] may have to be quite vigorous.

Individuals suffering from restless-legs syndrome (RL[S]) almost invariably suffer from periodic limb movement (s[ee] below) but not vice versa. Addiction to caffeine, uremia, a[nd] anemia should be considered as causes of leg discomfort.

Periodic-limb-movement disorder

Periodic-limb-movement disorder usually affects the legs. It [is] different to the sleep starts that occur at the onset of drow[si]ness prior to sleep. The toe extends and the ankle (and pos[si]bly knees and hips) flex a little. The movements occur eve[ry] 15–40 seconds and can be grouped into runs of half a minu[te] to an hour. Individuals may not be aware that these mov[e]ments are taking place, and can report unrefreshing sleep[,] insomnia, or daytime sleepiness. Bed partners may rep[ort] kicking. The movements can be sufficient to prevent sle[ep] reaching the deeper stages. If the EEG is examined, it can [be] seen that conscious awareness will not result from this type [of] disruption even though sleep itself is disturbed.

Patients with sleep apnea may move their limbs periodic[al]ly, but these movements often disappear when the sleep apn[ea] is treated. Also patients with epilepsy may have periodic li[mb] movements, but again these are different to those found [in] periodic-limb-movement disorder (PLMD).

Patients with RLS and PLMD may experience insomn[ia,] fatigue, and daytime sleepiness. The cause of the dayti[me] sleepiness is similar to that found in sleep apnea, meani[ng] that the limb movements are sufficient to disrupt sleep wit[h]out necessarily causing conscious waking. The sufferer [is] more likely to complain of insomnia if they do become co[n]scious during the limb movements.

Periodic limb movement has been associated with re[nal] disorders, and patients on dialysis may suffer more than mo[st.] There are also associations with iron-deficiency anem[ia]

muscle disorders, peripheral neuron disorders, diabetes, rheumatoid arthritis, chronic-fatigue syndrome, and fibromyalgia. Pregnancy often makes the disorder worse. Sleep polysomnography is most useful in confirming the diagnosis of RLS or PLMD and whether it is associated with any other sleep disorders.

Periodic limb movements and restless legs often occur together, and apart from being found in sleep apnea are also often found in narcolepsy. It is not clear why this should be. The current speculation is that these disorders involve damage to roughly the same areas of the brain.

Treatments currently include a number of different pharmacological approaches. Clonazepam or other benzodiazepines may be prescribed, or levodopa/carbidopa or bromocriptine, or various opioids (codeine, methadone, oxycodone, propoxyphene) may be tried before the right drug is found. Iron supplements, where a deficiency is noted, may be useful in elderly patients.

Circadian disorders

Sleeping difficulties that are related to problems with the biological clock are termed circadian disorders. The symptoms and problems are similar to those described in the sections on jet lag and shift-work but they do not disappear by themselves. The sufferer has a perpetual problem without treatment. These disorders often present themselves as insomnia or excessive daytime sleepiness. Without a diary it may not be immediately obvious that a circadian disorder is present. Prescription of sleeping pills is not helpful as it is often associated with increasing usage. Self-medication with alcohol and stimulants such as tobacco is common.

Phase delay, phase advance

Phase delay (also known as delayed-sleep-phase syndrome) is a problem that may be caused by the biological clock not being reset in the mornings. It causes progressively later and later bedtimes until social constraints, such as going to school or going to work, force the sleeper to get up. In the morning the sufferer is very drowsy because he or she is partially sleep-deprived, and because the circadian rhythm of alertness is still set for night-time sleep. As the day progresses they feel more and more alert, and this alertness is maintained in the evenings. Sufferers consistently complain of not being able to get to sleep at desirable bedtimes, and they often do not go to bed until after midnight, sometimes 02:00–03:00.

Absenteeism is a common result. Many individuals end up doing night-work as they cannot keep daytime jobs. The pattern of delayed sleep often develops early in life but becomes evident either at school or work. Individuals invariably sleep well on holiday, when there is no definite time to get up. This is a treatable disorder, but ideally it should be managed by a sleep disorders center. Chronotherapy, bright light and medications provide a wide variety of treatment possibilities.

Phase advance, which causes earlier and earlier bedtimes and getting up times, is also a clock disorder, often seen in the elderly. It is more likely to affect your social life than your work. Again, this is treatable by a sleep disorders center.

Non-24-hour sleep-awake syndrome, and irregular sleep-awake pattern

Two other clock disorders have been described: non-24-hour sleep-awake syndrome, and irregular sleep-awake pattern. In the former, sleep is delayed in a manner similar to phase-delay syndrome, but the 1–2 hour delays continue and are unremitting. The cycle length appears to be between 25 and 27 hours, and social and environmental cues fail to synchronize the sleep-awake pattern. Sleeping pills and stimulants rarely work. Many patients suffering from this syndrome give up trying to synchronize their sleep with socially acceptable times. Patients whose blindness has been caused by the complete destruction of the retina or severance of their optic nerves may suffer from this disorder as light-dark information is not being transmitted to the biological clock. Irregular sleep-awake pattern has no discernible cyclicity: neither 24-hour nor 90-minute cycles are evident. This can occur in elderly, possibly demented, and institutionalized patients.

Parasomnias

Parasomnias are usually undesirable or unusual behaviors associated with sleep. They occur exclusively within the

leep state and most are associated with either slow-wave
leep (deep sleep) or REM sleep. In terms of the sleep-
wake-clock systems, the sleep system is working but its
rchestration and control of other brain events is incom-
lete. The parasomnias are subdivided into arousal
isorders (such as sleepwalking), parasomnias associated
vith REM sleep, and other parasomnias.

rousal usually refers to physiological or cortical (brain)
ctivation. Originally, these disorders comprised sleepwalk-
ng (somnambulism), night terrors, nocturnal enuresis,
nd nightmare. Since then nocturnal enuresis and nightmare have been redefined. Sleepwalking and night terrors
)ccur in slow-wave sleep, whereas nightmares arise in REM
leep. Nocturnal enuresis can occur at any stage of sleep.

Arousal disorders

These disorders involve behaviors that are not fully con-
rolled by conscious awareness. In fact, conscious aware-
1ess may not return until after the behaviors have stopped.
There is invariably confusion, and little response to the
environment or people. It is very difficult to wake the
leeper and more often than not he or she does not recall
what was happening.

Sleepwalking usually begins abruptly. The sleeper sits up in
bed with a relatively blank expression on his or her face.
When the sleeper gets up he or she may adjust the bed and
pillow and walk around the room. Some of the movements
are clumsy and purposeless. However, many complex acts
have been described such as playing a musical instrument,
eating and drinking—even trying to phone someone.
Episodes usually last about 10 minutes.

Sleepwalking

Talking coherently is rare; a scream or inarticulate utter-
ances are more likely. Generally the person is very unresponsive, probably because they are still in slow-wave sleep,
or just out of slow-wave sleep. This stage is very deep and
much of the brain is involved in this activity that appears
not to be involved in any information processing. Waking
is difficult but not dangerous, although sleepwalkers may
resist attempts to wake up!

Despite the lack of response, sleepers do negotiate furniture relatively easily. Eating while sleepwalking seems to occur quite often. One case involved a woman who used to sleepwalk to the fridge and consume substantial amounts of food. Interestingly, she was also phobic to snakes, and treatment was eventually successful when a model snake was put in front of the fridge. This was sufficient to induce a change of mind and she went back to bed!

Most reported sleepwalking occurs between the age of 5 and adolescence, peaking around age 12. Sleepwalking does not usually go on beyond 12 years. Between 15 and 30 percent of children sleepwalk and 3 percent are frequent sleepwalkers. Both sexes are represented. In adults, there are suspicions that the occurrence of sleepwalking is greater than the 1 percent that is reported in most textbooks, but data is lacking. There are virtually no reports of sleepwalking in pregnant woment. There is a strong inheritance factor, with 80 percent of sleepwalkers having relatives who sleepwalk as well. Sleeptalking also occurs more often in sleepwalkers.

Stress, various medications, and alcohol can trigger bouts of sleepwalking. It is not a psychiatric disorder, but just reflects how the brain is organized and how various parts shut down (or not) during sleep. Children who sleepwalk can be triggered into walking by standing them up when they are deeply asleep.

Sleepwalking must be diagnosed accurately as other neurological disorders can cause similar activity. The general advice is to protect sleepwalkers because they can injure themselves. There are various medicines for the physician to try, and growing evidence that the activating SSRI class of antidepressants may be useful.

Finally, don't panic. It is very difficult to wake up someone who is sleepwalking, but it does them no harm if you must. Just don't expect to be thanked.

Night (sleep) terrors Night terrors are an abrupt waking out of slow-wave sleep (deep sleep), similar to sleepwalking, but are associated with a loud piercing scream, or some other loud noise.

Arguably, a night terror can be more frightening for the observer than the person experiencing it, as the sleeper rarely recalls the event. The scream can be associated with various repetitive movements: arms may flail about, there can be intense sweating, hair can stand up, the pupils may be dilated, and breathing may be rapid and shallow. The movements in a night terror might also involve the sleeper jumping out of bed, running out of the bedroom, and being injured in the process.

The whole episode can last about 15 minutes without the person ever really waking up. Mixtures of behavior can occur. The sleeper may be talking about what's happening one second and be fast asleep the next. Sufferers rarely recall the event the next day. For youngsters aged between 5 and 7, these episodes can occur roughly once a week. In younger children it may be as often as once a night. Two-thirds of children will have stopped by adolescence. Night terrors are unusual in adults, and there is a strong inheritance factor: 96 percent of sufferers have a family history.

The factors that trigger night terrors are similar to sleep-walking, namely stress, psychoactive compounds, and in adults alcohol. In children, night terrors do not imply that there is an underlying psychiatric or neurological problem, but simply reflect a maturing brain. In adults, however, since night terrors are rare, precipitating factors as well as underlying problems should be evaluated. As individuals suffering from night terrors seem fully in fright and flight mode, it is important to ensure that they don't injure themselves. There is no effective and safe treatment available.

There is another unusual disorder that may be linked to night terrors: unexplained nocturnal death syndrome. It is not clear whether this syndrome, which is most often found in South-east Asian refugees, arises in slow-wave sleep or REM sleep. Night terrors are associated with a massive increase in heart rate, and it has been postulated that this might trigger precipitous death in these individuals. Equally, in REM sleep, heart rate and respiration are less rigorously controlled than during wakefulness and other stages of sleep.

Confusional arousals

Other names for confusional arousals are sleep drunkenness or excessive sleep inertia. They typically occur out of slow-wave sleep but are much less dramatic than sleepwalking or night terrors. The person is often disoriented and will talk and think very slowly. There may be inappropriate behavior and inappropriate use of objects. Children may cry. These arousals are similar to the other disorders of arousal in that they occur mainly in children, decline with adolescence, and usually disappear in adulthood. Although disconcerting, they are harmless.

Parasomnias usually related to REM sleep

These behaviors are associated particularly with REM sleep. REM is usually a time of muscle paralysis (apart from breathing), a time when autonomic functions (breathing, heart rate, sweating, and other temperature regulation mechanisms) are less well regulated, and when the sexual apparatus is unrestrained. If awoken during REM sleep the individual usually reports bizarre stories with varying amounts of visual imagery. Most disorders involve a REM component failure.

Nightmares

Nightmares usually consist of long and complicated dreams that become more and more frightening. The awakening is associated with immediate recall of the dream and the person can be quite lucid about the experience—this contrasts strongly with night terrors.

Between 10–50 percent of children suffer from nightmares between the ages of 3 and 6. The incidence grows with age and then usually declines without active intervention, other than providing comfort and support. Dream content is variable and the anxiety that is provoked is purely subjective.

Nightmares occur in both girls and boys, but two to four times more women are affected in adulthood. Approximately 50 percent of adults admit to having an occasional nightmare. One percent of the population may have a nightmare every week.

Nightmares are frequently observed in those suffering from post-traumatic stress disorder (PTSD). This disorder

can arise after any traumatic event, both civilian and military, although military casualties have been studied most. Many Second World War veterans still suffer from anxiety dreams. In this older group, there may also be failures in breathing. The episodes of sleep apnea may cause an increase in autonomic and then emotional arousal that intrudes into the REM state. The emotional arousal then drives the content of the dream.

Treatment of nightmares varies. Medical practitioners may try prescribing drugs that reduce REM sleep with varying success. In PTSD cognitive and behavioral methods that help the individual in controlling the anxiety associated with the dream imagery can be quite successful.

The American neurologist Weir Mitchell reported two cases of sleep paralysis in 1876. As the name suggests, it involves waking up and not being able to move. It arises because of a mistiming between the systems that control the muscle paralysis of REM sleep and those that control wakefulness (*see page* 29). You wake up before you can move—it can be very frightening. It occurs rarely in normal individuals (once in a lifetime in 40–50 percent of the population), can run in families, is often associated with narcolepsy and may occasionally be seen in obstructive sleep apnea.

Sleep paralysis

The person afflicted can move the eyes and most of the muscles involved in breathing are unaffected—but some might be and this can give rise to feelings of suffocation. Most episodes only run for 1–2 minutes. Once experienced, most people realize if it happens again that sleep paralysis is not life-threatening. It can be more disturbing if it lasts longer, as the individual tends to drift in and out of dreams as well. In Victorian times sleep paralysis was regarded as so frightening by some that they asked for their wrists to be cut when they died, so as to avoid being buried alive. Sleep paralysis is similar to the medical condition cataplexy, and pharmacological treatments are similar.

REM behaviour disorder is almost the opposite to sleep paralysis, in that the mechanism controlling muscle paraly-

REM behavior disorder

sis does not work. Any movement in dreams is then acted out. The condition appears to occur in men more than women. It has only been described fully in recent years.

The number of episodes are rare to start with, but appear to increase over time. Patients may complain about the disorder to their doctor, but they are more likely to complain about daytime sleepiness first. Their partner may well be aware of their difficulties. The movements can be very dramatic, involving leaping and jumping out of bed. Some patients have been reported to have themselves tied down to their beds, or have themselves tied into sleeping bags so that they do not injure themselves or anyone else.

REM behavior disorder can be controlled using a particular benzodiazepine clonazepam. The reason for its peculiar efficacy is unknown.

Other parasomnias
Nocturnal enuresis

The Greek word to urinate is enuresis and it implies involuntary urination. Nocturnal enuresis just means wetting the bed at an age when this is not expected. Enuresis is subdivided into two types: secondary enuresis describes the onset of night-time wetting 3 or more months after night-time dryness has been established, whereas primary enuresis refers to someone who has never had a dry night. The age at which night-time dryness emerges depends on a number of factors: sex, pattern of wetting, and cultural background.

Toilet training usually follows a pattern of daytime control of urination, followed by daytime bowel control, followed by night-time bowel control and finally night-time bladder control. Control is achieved by the majority of children between 3 and 5 years old, but 15 percent of 5-year-olds still wet the bed. Generally, older children suffer from primary enuresis, because the development of control has never completed. However, secondary enuresis, once established, may take 1–2 years to abate. Young adults may also develop secondary enuresis. The incidence of enuresis in military populations is high: 20 percent.

Nocturnal enuresis should be regarded as a benign, although inconvenient, event. As always, some investigation is appropriate as it may be a symptom of a neurological disorder, but it should not be considered as a psychiatric disorder. It may be amenable to behavioral treatments, using conditioning devices that wake the sufferer when the urine triggers a sensor. Bladder training involves increasing fluids during the day so as to stretch the bladder, and reducing intake prior to sleep. There are also training programs to increase awareness of the sphincter muscles that control urination. The cause of the problem is still being investigated, but one of the strong possibilities is that not enough anti-diuretic hormone is secreted during the night. This hormone normally reduces urine production, so more is produced than the bladder can control.

The wicked shall see it and be grieved; he shall gnash with his teeth and melt away; the desire of the wicked shall perish. (Psalm 112 v. 10).

Sleep bruxism

Bruxism, or tooth-grinding, may start when teeth erupt, continue into adolescence, and may even occur in the elderly who have artificial teeth as well as the completely toothless. It occurs most in light sleep (stage 2) and can be accompanied by slow eye movements. It is often associated with stress. There are numerous hypotheses concerning the mechanisms involved and equally numerous treatments. Night-guards at least protect the teeth.

Chapter Eight

Using complementary therapies

This chapter outlines many of the complementary forms of healing and medicine that are said to affect sleep, or claim to treat insomnia or other sleep disorders. The danger in gathering together all these techniques in one chapter is that equal weight is apparently given to each one, but this is not intended. Chinese medicine and yoga, for example, have many thousands of years of tradition and practice behind them, whereas biorhythms, biofeedback, and hypnotherapy are relatively new to the healing professions.

Is it OK to use non-conventional techniques?

The answer is to consult with your doctor: there is no general advice. Your doctor should be able to advise you, assuming he or she knows the treatment. Most doctors take the view that alternative treatments are worth trying, provided they are not likely to do you any harm, and do not prevent you from using a conventional therapy that works.

Insomnia

Adult sleep is a learned behavior, and is an amalgamation of three controlling brain systems: sleep, awake and clock. For industrialized societies, the learning consists of identifying night-time (darkness) and the biological clock time so that the awake system runs down and the sleep system fires up. Whether someone sleeps on a particular night depends on his or her physical status (feeling well, ill, or in pain), mental status (worrying, depressed, or anxious), environment (noisy family, and so on), and how well learned is the association of darkness with sleep.

The chart on the following pages lists a variety of techniques claimed to have beneficial effects on sleep, making one wonder whether everything promotes sleep? This is quite likely. Many disturbances and disorders disrupt sleep, so many of these remedies may affect sleep by minimizing the disruption, rather than by any direct effect on sleep. Also the definition of insomnia is still in a process of refinement. But for the sufferer, none of this matters—if it works is far more important than why it works. The treatments featured in the chart can be grouped into the following categories.

Ingestions (herbs, minerals, and hormones)

Eating or drinking something for a sleep problem has been a "cure" from time immemorial. The reason for taking a particular herb, mineral, or hormone varies depending on which system of herbalism is used. Minerals that can be obtained from drug stores and health-food shops are also listed, including melatonin. Taking drugs, minerals, herbs, and the like, is rather like pouring gasoline over a car and hoping that some of it gets into the engine, so you should be wary of other effects than the one that is desired.

Thought management and anxiety relief

Worrying or arousing thoughts prevent sleep, so any method that absorbs your attention may allow sleep to cut in. Some methods were introduced earlier (see pages 119–127). Abdominal breathing, meditation, and yoga are direct forms. Interestingly, praying in any Eastern or Western religion (using mantras, tantras, chants, rosaries, and so on) may also have this effect.

Muscle and joint relaxation

Exercise, yoga, massage, the Alexander Technique, osteopathy, and many other treatments all have an impact on muscle and joint suppleness. The effect of tense muscles, whether caused by anxiety, poor posture or neurological disorders, is to disrupt sleep.

Pain control

Not only does pain interfere with sleep, but sleep disruption increases the intensity of pain. Many of the alternative techniques have a positive impact on pain, either by alleviating it or at least minimizing it.

Complementary therapies

Method	Description
Acupressure	A technique relying on the theory underlying acupuncture (*see below*), but using pressure instead of needles. Used for pain control.
Acupuncture	The discovery of acupuncture needles dating back to around 1,000 BC attests to the antiquity of Chinese medicine. Acupuncture is used for a wide range of problems, including back pain, and has been used as a form of anesthesia.
Alexander Technique	The Alexander Technique attempts to identify and release areas of unwanted muscle tension. It is an educational therapy aimed at improving physical and mental well-being by changes in posture. The hypothesis is that habitual bad coordination may lead to excess tension.
Aromatherapy	The use of fragrant oils has developed from the ancient use of aromatic herbs in Egypt, India, Greece, and the Arab world. Traditionally, essential oils have been used as stimulants, relaxants, antiseptics, and anti-inflammatories. They can alter mood and relieve stress.
Ayurveda	Ayurveda is an Asian medical system that has its beginnings more than 2,000 years ago. "Ayurveda" literally means "the science of longevity." It is an entire system, using herbal remedies, massage, yoga and meditation.
Bach Flower Remedies	Dr. Edward Bach developed a range of flower remedies in the 1930s. Morning Glory (*Ipomoea purpurea*) is the remedy used most often to treat sleeplessness.
Biofeedback	Biofeedback is useful for headaches, persistent backache, and muscle pain. Neurotherapy is a specific form of EEG biofeedback.
Biorhythms	Biorhythms have limited scientific support. They are completely different to the biological clock rhythms described earlier in this book.
Buteyko Method	A breathing re-conditioning program that treats asthma and other respiratory problems.
Chinese Herbal Medicine	A complete health system that looks at the body as a balance between the opposite energies of yin and yang. Traditional Chinese medicine includes herbal treatments for almost all known diseases as well as acupuncture, massage, diet, and exercise.

Complementary therapies

Method	Description
Chiropractic	A treatment with the emphasis on re-aligning and adjusting the spinal vertebrae. Manual treatment of many painful conditions, including back pain, sports injuries, and asthma.
Colon Hydrotherapy	An infusion of purified water into the colon is said to cleanse and detoxify the inner body. Claimed to be useful in treating headaches, backache, constipation, and diarrhea.
Counseling	This includes psychotherapy and hypnotherapy. Used for thought management and anxiety relief.
Devices	Many devices are used in conventional medicine now, primarily to improve breathing, and some of these have already been mentioned (nasal dilators, jaw-extension devices, and nasal continuous-airway-pressure devices). Isocones are rubber cones that can be strapped onto the wrists to provide stimulation of the classical acupuncture points.
Feng Shui	Feng shui is said to be the practice of living harmoniously with the energy of the surrounding environment. Sleep along a north-south axis, aligning yourself with the earth's magnetic field. If you were born in autumn or winter your bed should face south, and if you were born in spring or summer your bed should face north.
Hands-on Healing	Generally, hands-on healing and faith healing propose that the mind guides the body and faith healers empower the mind, allowing it to channel its energy to either improve body function or make the body feel better.
GDS Method	This is a holistic treatment and preventative approach to a wide range of musculoskeletal problems.
Hellerwork	Founded by Joseph Heller who works from a center at Mt. Shasta, California. It is based on movement education as well as deep tissue manipulation. Used for muscle and joint relaxation.
Herbal Remedies	• CALIFORNIAN POPPY (*Eschscholzia california*) Used as a sedative and hypnotic, with a reputation for being a non-addictive alternative to the opium poppy.

Complementary therapies

Method	Description
Herbal Remedies (cont.)	• CHAMOMILE (*Chamaemelum nobile*) Chamomile tea is a gentle sedative that can help anxiety and promote restful sleep. Chamomile tea bags reduce eye inflammation and refresh tired eyes.
	• HOPS (*Humulus lupulus*) The flower inflorescence is used extensively for the treatment of sleeplessness, except for anyone suffering from depression.
	• JAMAICAN DOGWOOD (*Piscidia erythrina*) This is regarded as a strong remedy for sleeplessness (it is also used as a fish poison), particularly if the sleeplessness is caused by pain.
	• LADY'S SLIPPER (*Cypripedium pubescens*) The root is recommended for treatment of anxiety associated with sleeplessness.
	• LAVENDER (*Lavendula officinalis*) Lavender oil is used in aromatherapy for anxiety, insomnia, and depression.
	• MULLEIN (*Verbascum thapsus*) Infused as a tea to stimulate the respiratory system and help with difficult breathing; good for asthma, bronchitis and sinus problems.
	• PASSION FLOWER (*Passiflora incarnata*) The dried leaves are used for treating intransigent insomnia.
	• PEPPERMINT (*Mentha piperita*) Peppermint is said to promote relief from symptoms that may interfere with normal sleep. It is used to treat nervousness, insomnia and dizziness.
	• SCOT'S PINE (*Pinus sylvestris*) The twigs are soaked in water then added to bath water to ease fatigue and sleeplessness.
	• SKULLCAP (*Scutellaria lateriflora*) A herb thought to relax nervous tension and counteract sleeplessness. It was entered in the US Pharmacopoeia in 1863 as a tranquilizer.
	• ST JOHN'S WORT (*Hypericum perforatum*) Used as a sedative. This herb has similar properties to older antidepressants and takes 2–4 weeks to exert its effect.

Complementary therapies

Method	Description
Herbal Remedies (cont.)	• VALERIAN (*Valeriana officinalis*) Valerian is recognized as a sedative, and can be found in conventional medical formularies. Herbalists recommend it for nervousness, anxiety, insomnia, headache and intestinal cramps.
	• WILD LETTUCE (*Lactuca virosa*) Used to treat insomnia, restlessness, and over-excitability in children, as well as adults. It has also been used to relieve pain.
Homeopathy	A complete system of complementary medicine based on the idea that a substance that produces a set of symptoms comparable to those present in a disorder can be used to treat the disorder. The remedies are prepared from extracts of plants, minerals, animal and human secretions and tissues.
Hydrotherapy	This therapy is claimed to stimulate blood circulation, draw out heat, and provide support while exercising. It is occasionally used for insomnia.
Hypnotherapy	Ancient Egyptians and Greeks are said to have used healing trances. African and American tribal cultures also use drumming and dancing for hypnotic effects. Using trances to implant suggestions for self-cure has been used by the healing professions since the eighteenth century.
Kinesiology	The study of muscle movement. Used for muscle and joint relaxation.
Light therapy and bright light	Light therapy, as currently used, refers to treatments that increase production of Vitamin D, thus aiding absorption of some minerals. Bright light can be used to reset the biological clock.
Minerals	• MAGNESIUM A lack of magnesium is associated with early morning awakening. Magnesium supplement has been shown to improve sleep in people with magnesium deficiency.
	• ZINC, COPPER, IRON AND CALCIUM Zinc, copper, iron, anc calcium supplements have been associated with improvements in sleep.
Naturopathy	Naturopathic medicine is a natural approach to health and healing that recognizes the integrity of the whole person. It emphasizes the treatment of disease through the stimulation, enhancement, and support of the intrinsic healing capacity of the person.

Complementary therapies

Method	Description
Osteopathy	This is the treatment of painful joints and soft tissue through muscle relaxation and joint articulation techniques.
Pharmaceutical and natural substances	• ASPIRIN Peter Hauri (Mayo Clinic) has reported that some insomniacs who wake late in the night benefit from aspirin taken in the evening, but the effect is transient.
	• AMINO ACIDS Arginine, lysine and ornithine have all been used to control sleep and wakefulness but their use as remedies is not substantiated. Tryptophan, once popular as a sleep aid, is used mainly by the brain to manufacture serotonin, and can be found in many health-food stores.
	• MELATONIN Melatonin is a brain hormone that provides information for the brain and body that it is dark. In adults it is secreted regularly during the night. It is available as a health-food supplement in some countries and is banned in others. Its use may be confined to chronobiological disorders, and possibly jet lag.
	• VITAMINS Vitamins B6, B12 and folic acid are associated with control of sleep. B3 has been found to be useful in insomnia and depression.
Psychotherapy	Psychotherapy usually refers to psychoanalytic or psychodynamic therapy, but can also refer to other pyschological treatments that have not been endorsed by professional associations.
Seichem	Seichem is a complete healing system. It is claimed to benefit those suffering from stress-related conditions. Seichem alleviates pain associated with arthritis, migraine, injuries and other deep-rooted illness.
Shiatsu	Shiatsu is a Japanese massage technique which literally means finger presssure. It promotes deep relaxation, and so can help relieve stress.
Tai Chi	Tai Chi is an ancient Chinese exercise system for body, mind and spirit— a form of "moving meditation." Its practice improves health, vitality and well-being.
Yoga	Yoga is an ancient form of exercise. Successful practice of yoga can reduce stress and increase suppleness, both of which can benefit sleep.

Resources

Website

Further information, internet links, updates on diary interpretation and discussion and comparison of diaries can be found in the *Insomnia Kit* forum. This is hosted by www.neuronic.com. If you have problems reaching the *Insomnia Kit* site, e-mail either InsomniaKit@neuronic.com or InsomniaKit@btinternet.com.

Useful addresses

National Center on Sleep Disorders Research
PO Box 30105, Bethesda
Maryland 20824–0105
This is also the address for the National Heart, Lung and Blood Institute (NHLBI), the National Institute of Health, and the NHLBI Information Centre.

American Sleep Disorders Association
1610 14th Street NW, Suite 300
Rochester MN 55901
Phone: (507) 287-6006
Fax: (507) 287-6008
This is a professional medical association representing practitioners of sleep medicine and sleep research. Contact them to find out the centers in your local area.

The Canadian Sleep Society/
Société Canadienne du Sommeil
(CSS/SCS)
3080 Yonge Street, Suite 5055
Toronto, Ontario M4N 3N1
Phone: (416) 483-6260
Fax: (416) 483-7081

Sleep/Wake Disorders Canada
3080 Yonge Street, Suite 5055
Toronto, Ontario M4N 3N1
Phone: (416) 483-9654
Fax: (416) 483-7081
E-mail: swdc@globalserve.net

Narcolepsy Network
277 Fairfield Avenue, Suite 310B
Fairfield NJ 07004

Restless Legs Syndrome Foundation
4410 19th Street NW, Suite 201
Rochester MN 55901

National Sleep Foundation
729 15th Street NW, Fourth Floor
Washington DC 20005

Ohio Sleep Medicine and
Neuroscience Institute
(Attn: Helmut S. Schmidt, M.D./
Betty Hammonds)
4975 Bradenton Avenue
Dublin OH 43017
Phone: (614) 766-0773
Fax: (614) 766-2599

American Sleep Apnea Association
2025 Pennsylvania Avenue NW,
Suite 905
Washington DC 20006

Society for Light Treatment and
Biological Rhythms
10200 West 44th Avenue, Suite 304
Wheat Ridge CO 80033–2840

Society for the Study of Dreams
PO Box 1600
Vienna VA 22183

Sleep Disorders Dental Society
11676 Perry Highway
Building #1, Suite 1204
Wexford PA 15090

American Holistic Medical
Association
6728 Old McLean Village Drive
McLean VA 22101–3906
Tel: (703) 556-9728

Fax: (703) 556-8729
E-mail: HolistMed@aol.com

American Holistic Health
Association
PO Box 17400
Anaheim CA 92817–7400
Phone: (714) 779-6152
E-mail: ahha@healthy.net

Further reading

Devereux, Charla and Fran Stockel, *The Meditation Kit*. Boston: Journey Editions, 1997.

Kleitman, Nathaniel, *Sleep and Wakefulness*. Chicago: University of Chicago Press, 1987 (1st edition 1939).

Mendelson, W. B., *Human Sleep: Research and Clinical Care*. New York and London: Plenum Medical Book Company, 1987.

Needham, Alex, *The Stress Management Kit*. Boston: Journey Editions, 1996.

Oswald, Ian, *Sleep*. London: Penguin, 1980 (4th edition).

Powell, Cherith and Greg Forde, *The Self-Hypnosis Kit*. New York: Penguin Studio Books, 1995.

Stampi, Claudio (editor), *Why We Nap: Evolution, Chronobiology, and Functions of Polyphasic and Ultrashort Sleep* (workshop on polyphasic and ultrashort sleep-wake patterns). Boston: Birkhäuser, 1992.

Index

*Page numbers in **bold** refer to diagrams and charts*

Acknowledgements

Along with many UK sleep researchers, my introduction to sleep was Ian Oswald's book *Sleep* (see "Further reading" page 157). This is still an excellent read as much of the contemporary research has moved in a different direction. Another classic book that has not aged is Nathaniel Kleitman's *Sleep and Wakefulness* (see "Further reading"). Both of these have been a source of inspiration for many years.

Technical prowess and expertise is required to get good sleep recordings. Over the years I have been lucky to have always had excellent technical team leaders—Bobby James and Jane Jones—to direct superb technical staff. Technicians are rarely seen as they spend a lot of the time working at night, but without them there would be little scientific or clinical advance.

I have been involved with a number of different patient groups but I have to thank UK's Sleep Matters and the Finnish insomnia group—in particular, Ruth Koskinen, (go to the www.neuronic.com website for more information) to remind me how difficult life is for a sleep-disordered patient and especially a chronic insomniac.

The rulers were originally developed as a response to an unrecognized clinical need. Most primary care physicians in most countries do not get much education on sleep and its disorders, and have to manage the health of their patients with what they know. The rulers provided a mechanism through which I could help advise both doctor and patient. I should also acknowledge Eddison Sadd (the whole team) for extending the availability of the sleep ruler to a wide audience. I would also like to thank my editor Alexa Stace.

Finally, the web should also be acknowledged. The ability to access tremendous volumes of information remotely, and to directly recall books from the British Library was a tremendous help in the production of this book.

EDDISON • SADD EDITIONS

Project Editor............................ Tessa Monina
Editor... Alexa Stace
Proofreader............................... Slaney Begley
Indexer...................................... Dorothy Frame

Art Director.............................. Elaine Partington
Senior Art Editor..................... Pritty Ramjee
Illustrator.................................. Steve Rawlings
Line artworks............................ Julie Carpenter

Production.................................. Karyn Claridge and
                                                    Charles James

Eddison Sadd would like to thank Cherith Powell for her help in recording the tape, Sarah Howerd for the loan of the waves, and EMR for production.